HUMAN BODY
FACTS
FOR SHARP MINDS

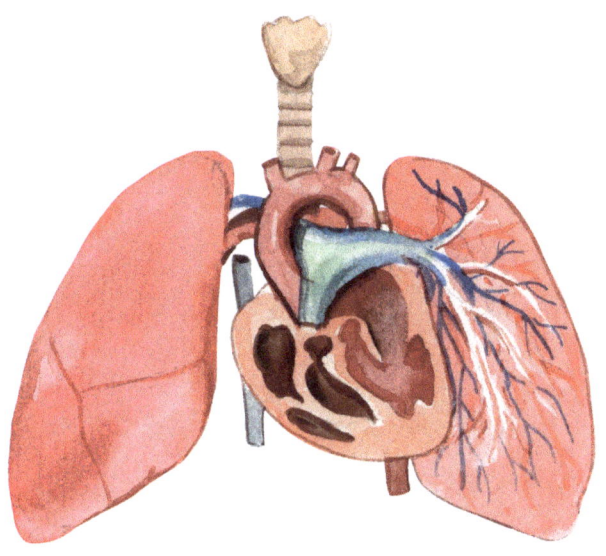

A wonderful book for the whole Family!

Copyright © 2023 by Sharp Minds Learning

ALL RIGHTS RESERVED

No part of this book may be reproduced, stored in a retrieval system, or transmitted in any form or by any means, electronic, mechanical, photocopying, recording, scanning, or otherwise, without the prior written permission of the publisher.

INTRODUCTION

Embark on an enlightening journey through the extraordinary landscape of the human body with "Human Body Facts for Sharp Minds." In this meticulously crafted exploration, we present facts and offer an immersive experience where each revelation is accompanied by vivid illustrations that bring to life the intricate workings of our anatomy.

Prepare to be captivated by 70 fascinating facts, each unlocking the mysteries of our physical existence. From the microscopic wonders within our cells to the grand orchestration of our organ systems, this book is a visual and intellectual feast for the curious mind.

As you turn the pages, anticipate a visual symphony of images expertly curated to complement the richness of the accompanying facts. Whether you're a seasoned enthusiast of human biology or a casual learner eager to absorb the marvels of the human form, this book is your key to unlocking the door to knowledge.

Join us on this enlightening journey, where each fact is not just a piece of information but a revelation that unveils the beauty and complexity of our vessel. "Human Body Facts for Sharp Minds" invites you to expand your understanding, enrich your appreciation, and satisfy your curiosity about the miraculous machine that is the human body. Get ready for an immersive experience that celebrates the wonders within each of us.

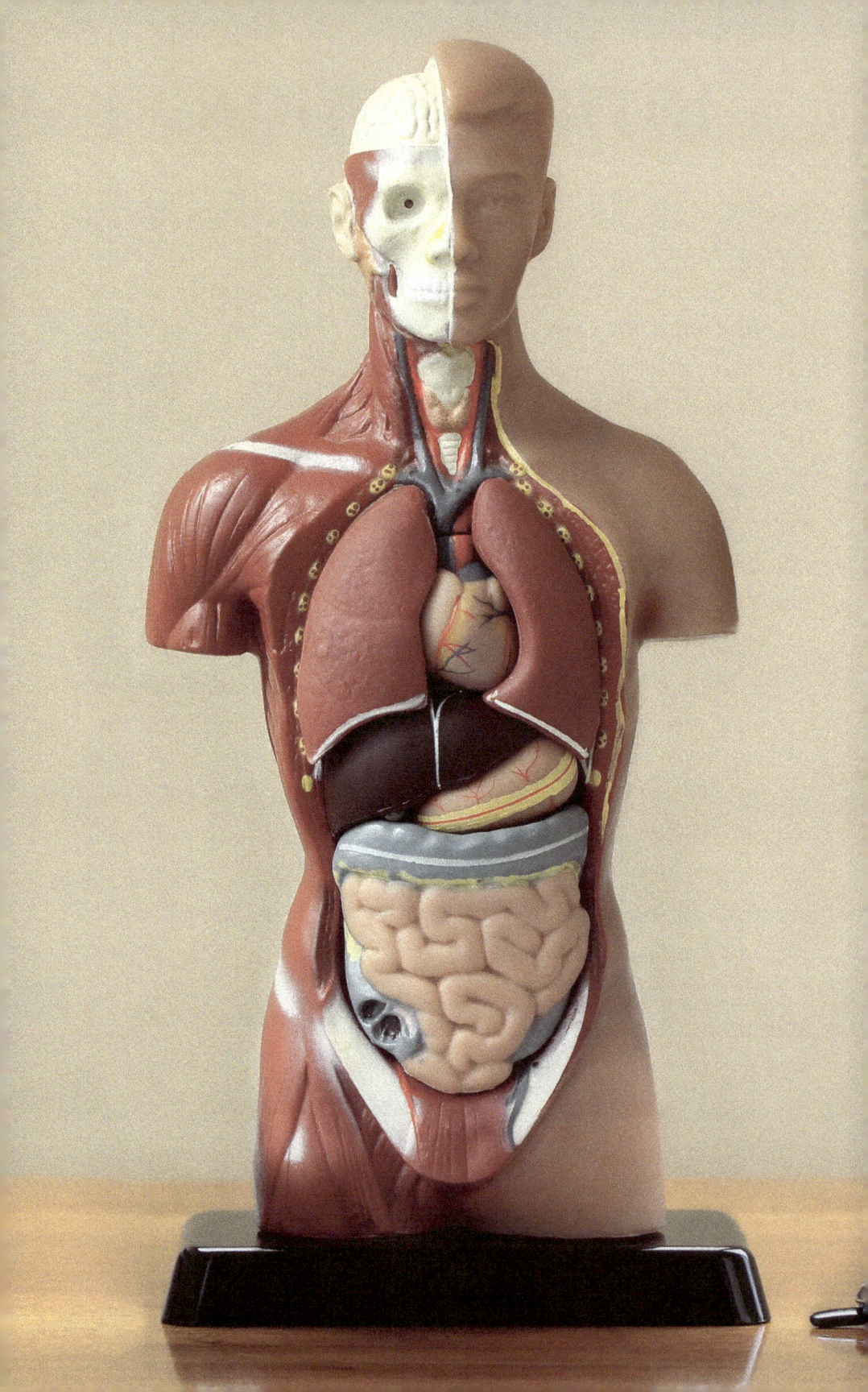

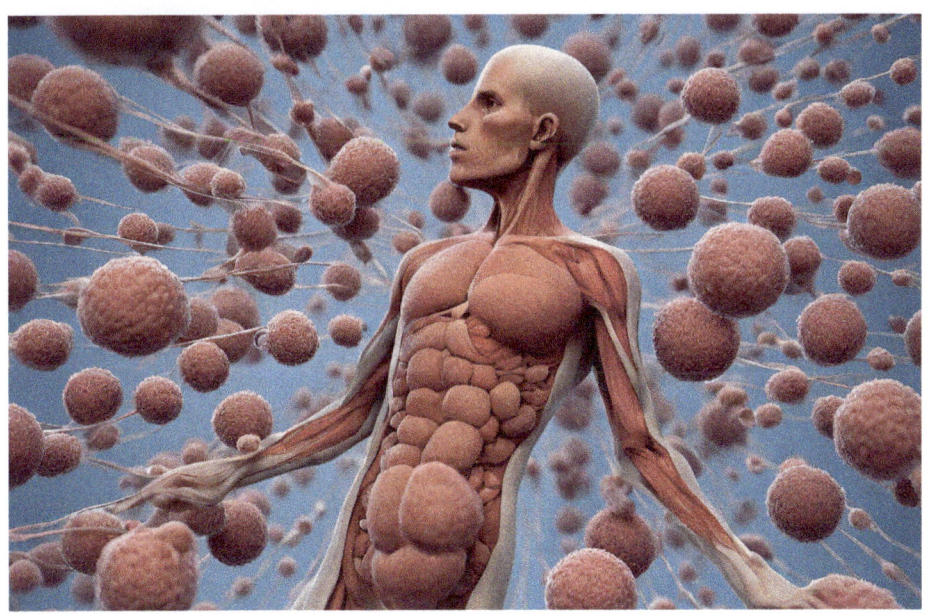

Fact#1

The human body is made up of around 37.2 trillion individual cells.

The human body is a complex system made up of a vast number of cells. These cells are the basic building blocks of life, and each one has a specific function. The human body has many different types of cells, ranging from blood to skin and nerve cells. In total, it is estimated that there are approximately 37.2 trillion individual cells in the human body. This huge number of cells allows our bodies to perform the many functions necessary for life, such as breathing, digesting food, and fighting off infections. Each cell has its unique role, and their collective efforts allow our bodies to perform tasks, heal, and adapt to an ever-changing environment, making them the building blocks of life itself.

Fact# 2

The human brain is the most energy-consuming organ in the body.

The human brain is indeed the most energy-consuming organ in the body. Despite accounting for only about 2% of a person's body weight, the brain consumes a disproportionately high amount of energy. On average, the human brain uses about 20% of the body's total energy expenditure. This high energy consumption is primarily due to the brain's continuous and complex activities, including thinking, processing information, maintaining neural connections, and regulating various bodily functions. Glucose is the brain's primary source of energy, and the brain requires a steady supply of glucose and oxygen to function properly. This high metabolic demand underscores the importance of a healthy diet and adequate blood flow to the brain for optimal cognitive function and overall brain health.

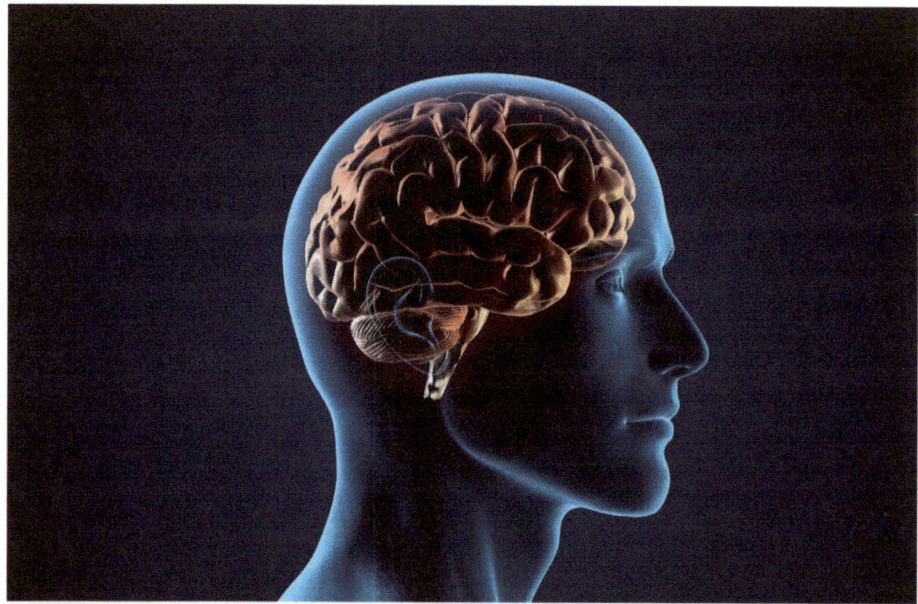

Fact# 3

Did you know that the cornea of the eye does not contain any blood vessels?

The cornea, which is the eye's clear front surface, is unique because it has no blood vessels. This particular feature is essential for maintaining the cornea's clarity, which is crucial for proper vision. Unlike other body parts, the cornea gets its oxygen and nutrients directly from the air and tears covering its surface rather than from blood vessels. Nutrients and oxygen are supplied to the cornea through diffusion from the tear fluid on the outside and the aqueous humour, a clear, watery fluid in the front part of the eye. Because the cornea is avascular, light can pass through it quickly and reach the retina at the back of the eye, where the visual process begins.

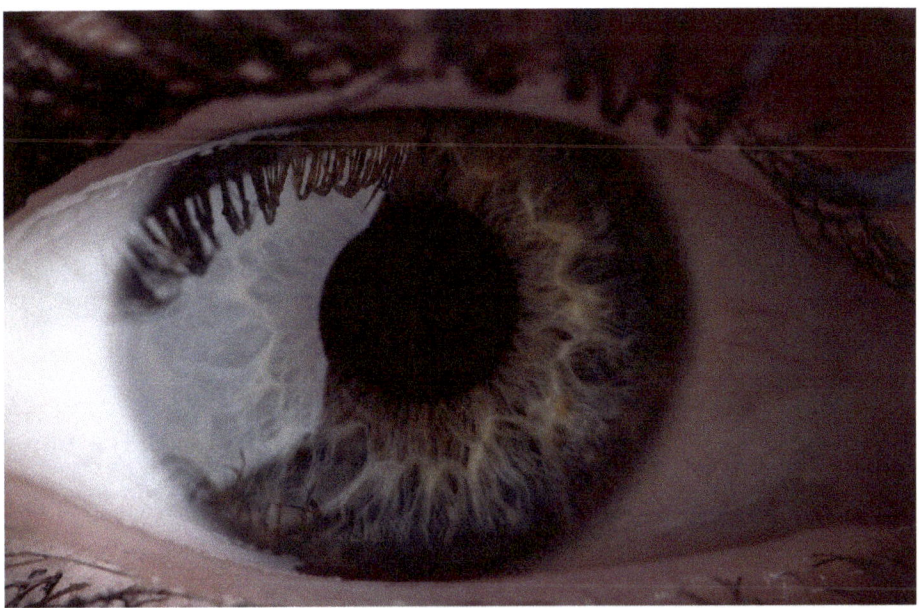

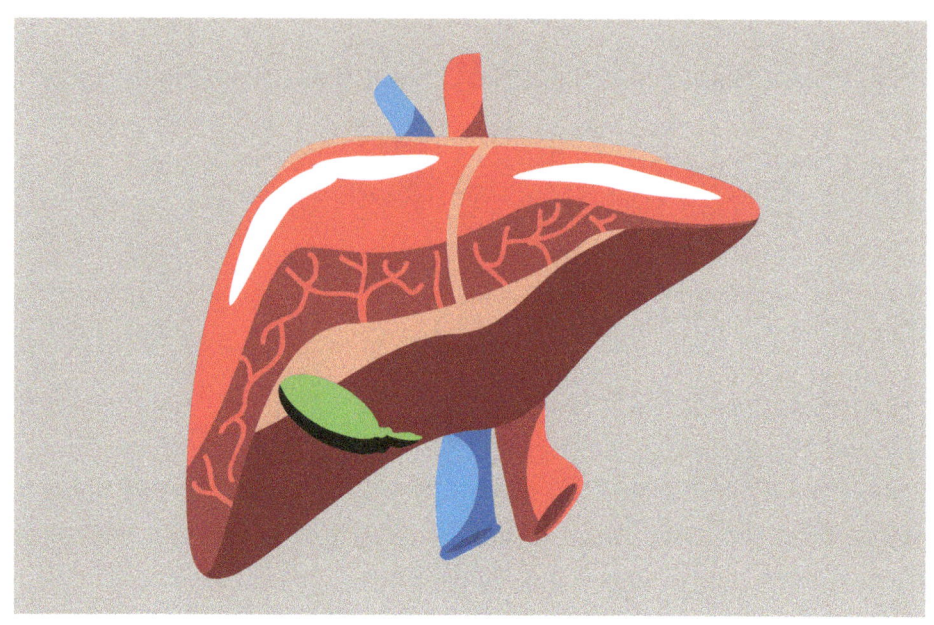

Fact# 4

Do you know what the largest internal organ in the human body is?

The liver is the largest internal organ in the human body, and it is renowned for its incredible ability to regenerate. This regenerative capacity is essential for the liver to perform its functions. When a part of the liver is removed due to surgery or injury, the remaining healthy tissue can regenerate and restore the liver to its normal size and function over time. The liver's regenerative capability is attributed to the presence of hepatocytes, which are the functional cells in the liver. These hepatocytes can divide and multiply to replace any damaged or lost tissue. However, chronic alcohol abuse or certain liver diseases can cause severe and repeated damage to the liver, leading to scarring or cirrhosis, which can limit its regenerative potential.

Fact# 5

Every person has a distinct fingerprint that is unique to them.

Each person has unique ridges and furrows on their fingertips, known as fingerprints. Even identical twins, who share the same genetic makeup, have different fingerprints. This uniqueness makes fingerprints a valuable tool for personal identification and forensic purposes. Fingerprints are formed during fetal development and are influenced by genetic and environmental factors. Genetic factors largely determine the ridges and patterns on the fingertips. Still, their exact formation is also influenced by factors such as blood flow, pressure, and contact with the amniotic fluid in the womb. Fingerprint identification is widely used in law enforcement, security, and various identification systems because of its reliability and uniqueness.

Fact# 6

The human heart can beat more than 100,000 times a day.

An adult's average resting heart rate is typically between 60 and 100 beats per minute. When you calculate this over the course of a day, it amounts to well over 100,000 heartbeats. The heart's continuous beating is essential for pumping oxygenated blood throughout the body to deliver nutrients and remove waste products. It works tirelessly to ensure that all the body's cells and organs receive the oxygen and nutrients they need to function properly. The heart rate can vary based on physical activity, stress, and age. Regular exercise and a healthy lifestyle help maintain a strong and efficient heart, potentially reducing the risk of heart-related health issues.

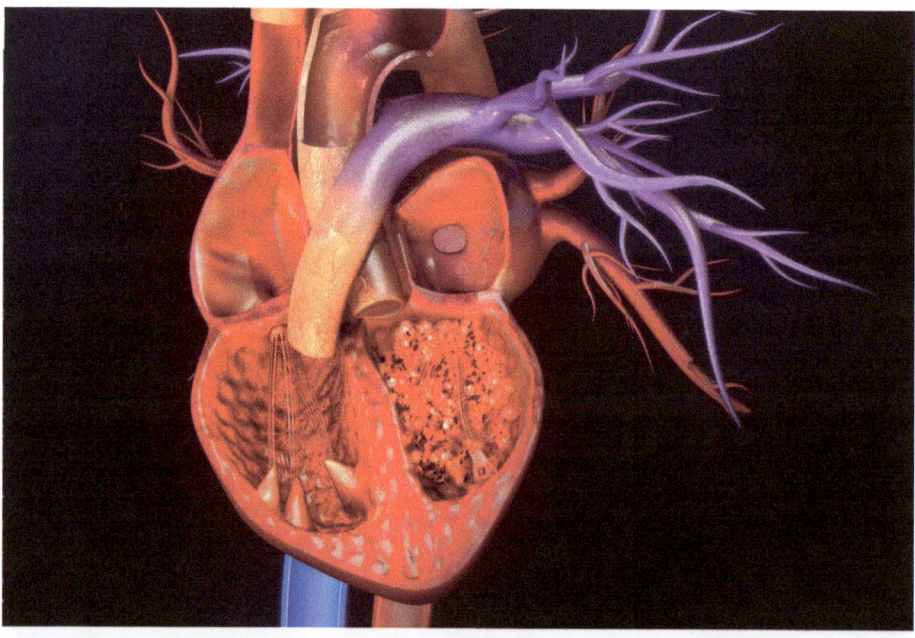

Fact# 7

Did you know that newborns have more bones than adults?

A full-grown adult typically has around 206 bones, but an infant is born with a greater number of bones, usually around 300. These extra bones in infants result from the natural development and growth process. As a person grows, some of these bones gradually fuse. The process of bone fusion is known as ossification. By the time an individual reaches adulthood, many smaller bones in the infant's body have merged to form larger, more stable bones. This fusion reduces the total number of bones to the adult average of approximately 206. The exact number of bones in the human body can vary slightly from person to person due to individual differences and the presence of extra or accessory bones in some cases.

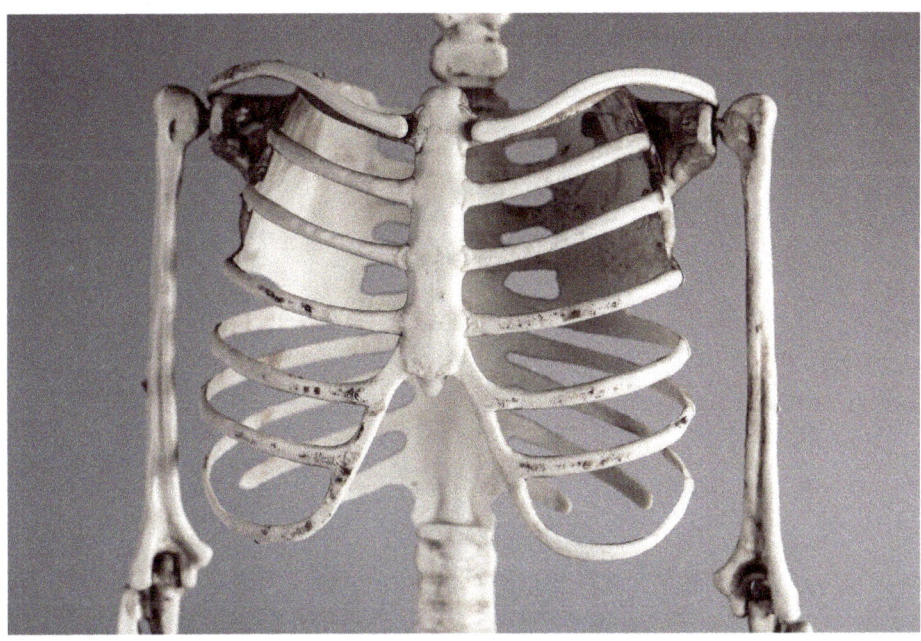

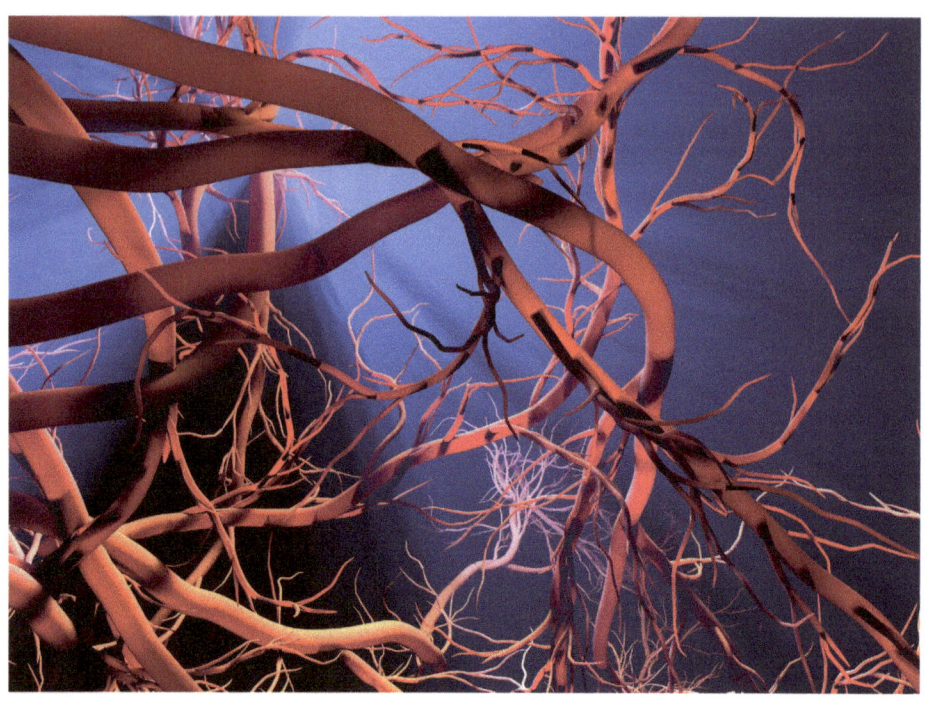

Fact# 8

Believe it or not, human blood vessels, if stretched out, would circle the Earth.

If you took all the blood vessels in the human body, including arteries, veins, and capillaries, and stretched them out end to end, they would be long enough to circle the Earth 2.5 times. This is a testament to the extensive network of blood vessels that is required to supply oxygen and nutrients to every cell and organ in the human body. The exact length of the circulatory system can vary from person to person, but it's generally estimated to be in the range of 60,000 to 100,000 miles (96,560 to 160,934 kilometres). This incredible length is necessary to ensure that blood can reach every body part, whether small or remote, to support vital physiological functions.

Fact# 9

Did you know that there are billions of teeny-tiny bacteria chillin' in your mouth right now?

The human mouth is home to a diverse and complex ecosystem of microorganisms, including bacteria. It is estimated that a typical human mouth can contain billions of bacteria. The specific number and composition of these bacteria can vary among individuals and are influenced by factors such as oral hygiene, diet, and genetics. While the presence of bacteria in the mouth is normal, maintaining good oral hygiene through practices like regular brushing and flossing is important to keep the bacterial population in check and prevent oral health issues such as cavities and gum disease. A balanced and diverse oral microbiome is a crucial component of oral health.

Fact# 10

The only jointless bone in the human body is the hyoid bone, located in the neck.

The hyoid bone is the only bone in the human body that is not connected to any other bone. It is a U-shaped bone located in the neck, just above the larynx (voice box) and below the mandible (lower jaw). The hyoid bone is an anchor for several muscles involved in swallowing and speaking. One of its unique features is that the hyoid bone is not directly connected to any other bone in the body. It plays a crucial role in various functions, including swallowing, phonation (speech), and maintaining the shape and position of the upper respiratory tract. Its mobility and position are essential for proper vocalization and complex swallowing.

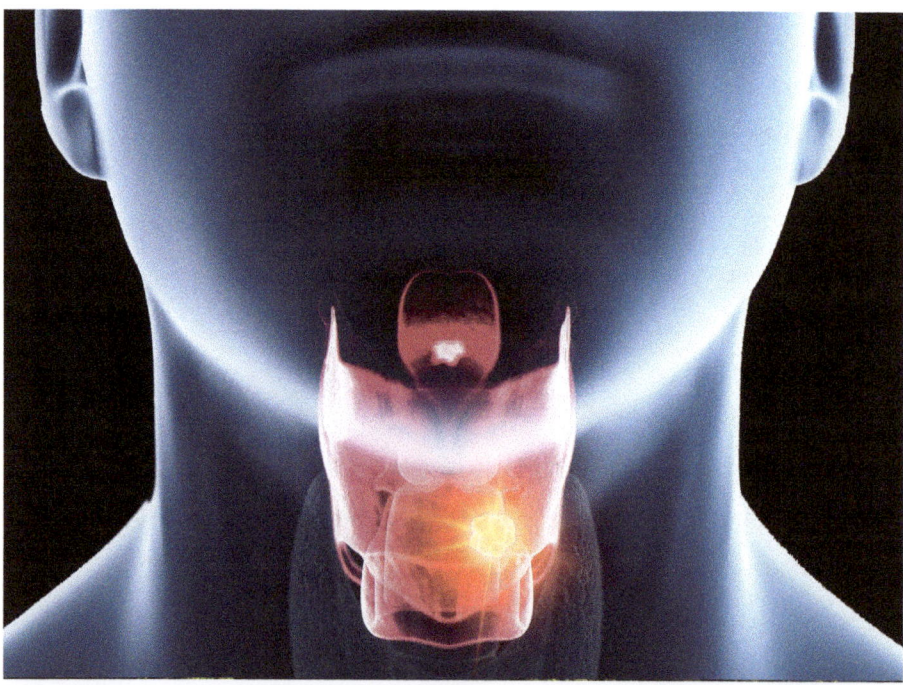

Fact# 11

Our sniffers are no joke! We humans can detect a whopping 10,000 distinct smells.

Our ability to distinguish between different odours, also known as olfactory discrimination, is a remarkable aspect of our sensory perception. The human olfactory system is a complex and highly sensitive sensory system that enables us to perceive and differentiate an astonishing variety of odours. Researchers estimate that humans can distinguish between approximately 10,000 different odours, which showcases the incredible capacity of our sense of smell. The intricate network of olfactory receptors in the nasal epithelium makes this possible. When we encounter different substances in our environment, volatile molecules are released into the air, and our olfactory receptors detect these molecules.

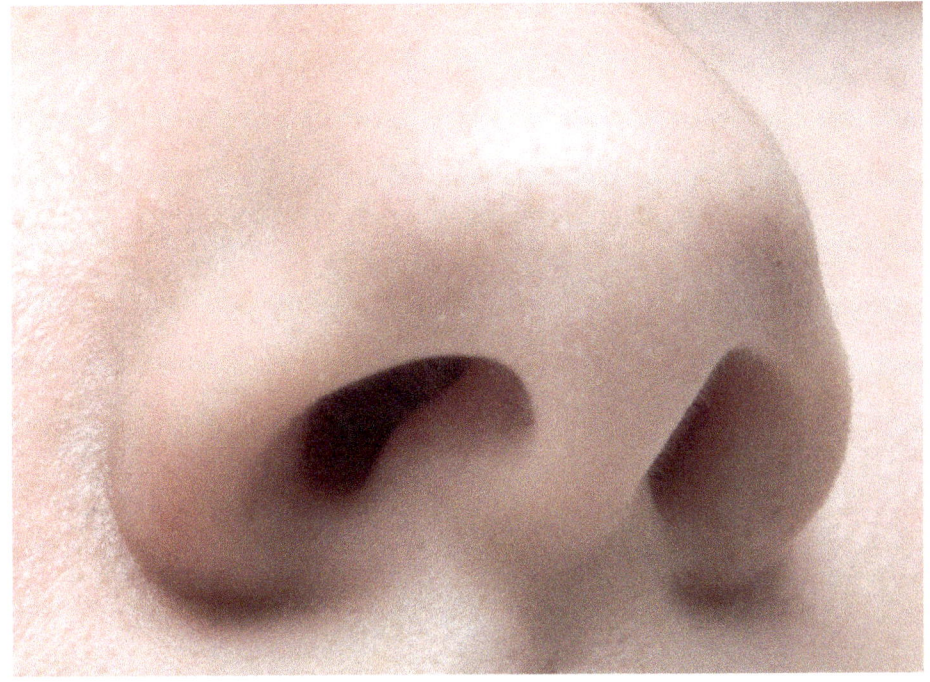

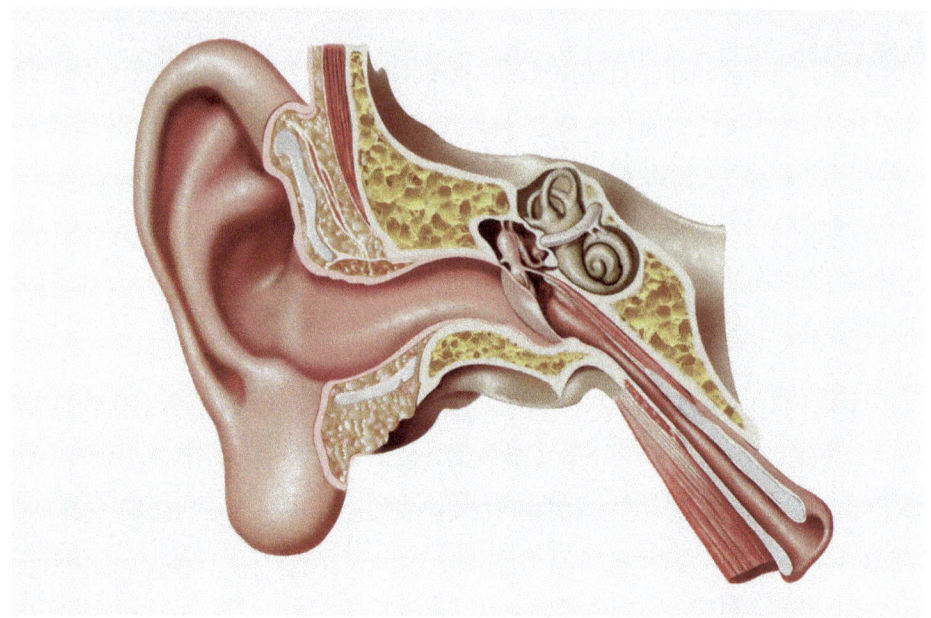

Fact# 12

The smallest bone in the human body is the stapes bone in the ear.

The stapes, which is also known as the stirrup bone, is the tiniest bone in the human body, measuring just about 0.1 inches. It is one of three minuscule bones located within the middle ear, collectively known as the ossicles, which are crucial for hearing. The stapes bone is situated in the middle ear, specifically in the oval window, and it plays a pivotal role in transmitting sound vibrations from the outer ear to the inner ear. Despite its small size, the stapes bone is essential for the proper functioning of the auditory system. Its precise and delicate structure enables it to effectively transmit sound waves, magnifying and transmitting them to the inner ear, where they are further processed into electrical signals that the brain can interpret as sound.

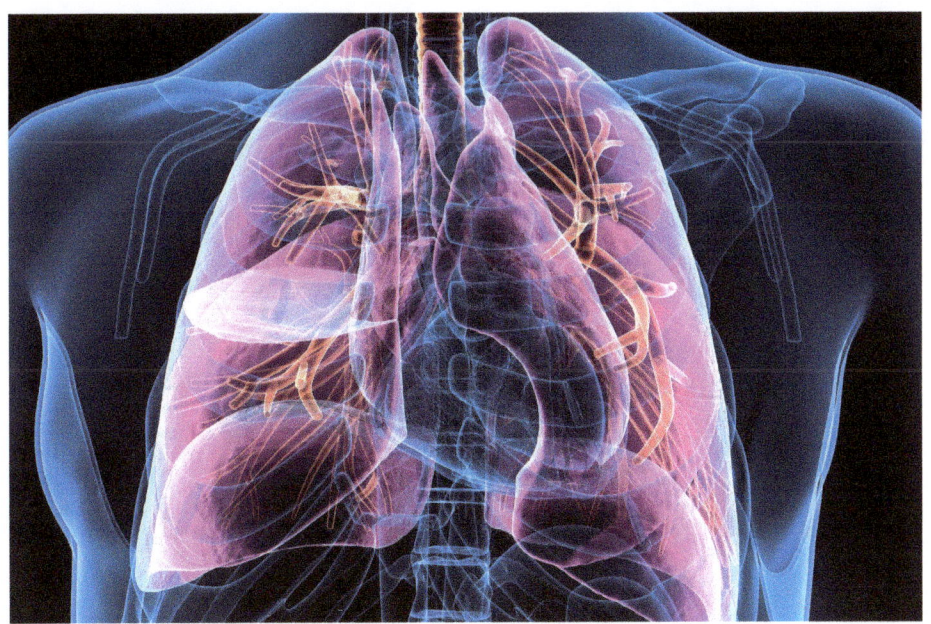

Fact# 13

Did you know that the left lung is actually smaller than the right lung?

The left lung is indeed smaller than the right lung in humans, and one of the reasons for this size difference is to accommodate the space needed for the heart. The human heart is located in the chest cavity between the two lungs and is positioned slightly to the left of the centre of the chest. This positioning of the heart means that the left lung is smaller to make room for the heart and allow it to function properly. The left lung has two lobes, while the right lung has three. The left lung also has a concavity on its surface called the cardiac notch, a space where the heart fits. This asymmetry is a natural adaptation to ensure the heart has enough room to expand and contract as it pumps blood throughout the body.

Fact# 14

The human body has the ability to heal broken bones.

This phenomenon is known as bone remodelling or bone regeneration. When a bone breaks, the body initiates a natural healing process. Initially, there is inflammation at the fracture site, followed by the formation of a soft callus made of fibrous tissue and, eventually, the remodelling of this tissue into hard bone tissue. During the remodelling phase, the body can strengthen the bone by depositing additional mineralized material, such as calcium, into the healing bone. Factors that can influence the strength of the healed bone include the type and location of the fracture, the individual's age and overall health, and the quality of the medical care and treatment received. Adequate nutrition, physical therapy, and proper medical care can optimize healing, potentially leading to a more robust, healed bone.

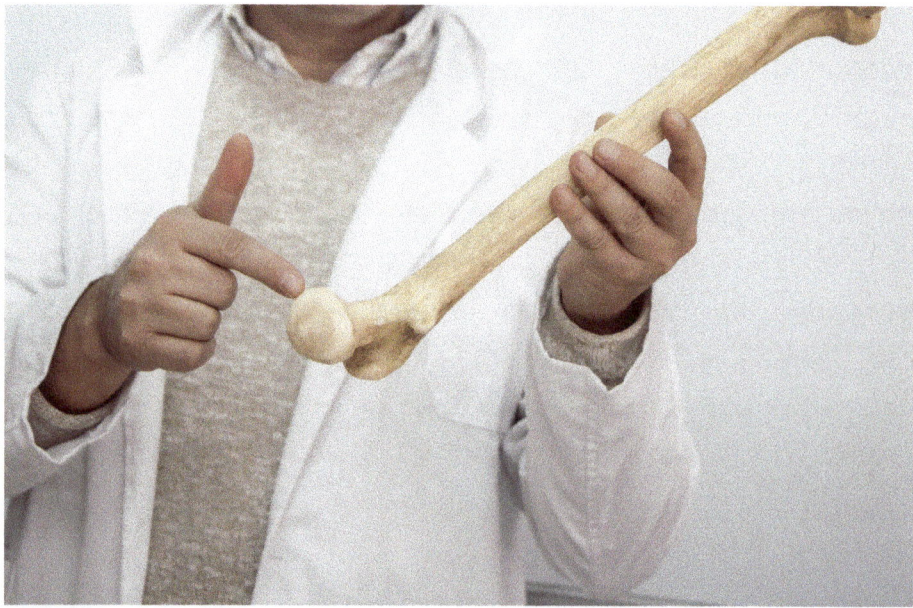

Fact# 15

Did you know that the thickest skin on your body is on the soles of your feet, while the thinnest is on your eyelids?

Skin thickness is measured in millimetres, and it is thickest on the soles of the feet and palms of the hands, where it can be several millimetres thick. This thickness is due to the presence of a thicker layer of epidermis and a substantial amount of keratin, which provides protection and durability for these high-use areas. Conversely, the skin on the eyelids is among the thinnest on the body, measuring only a fraction of a millimetre. The skin in this area is delicate and lacks the same degree of protective tissue, making it particularly sensitive.

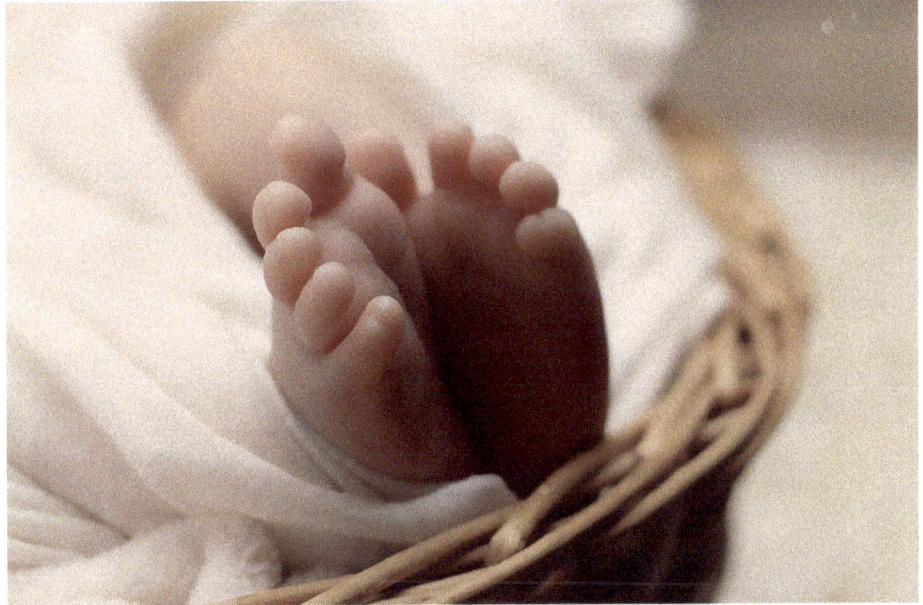

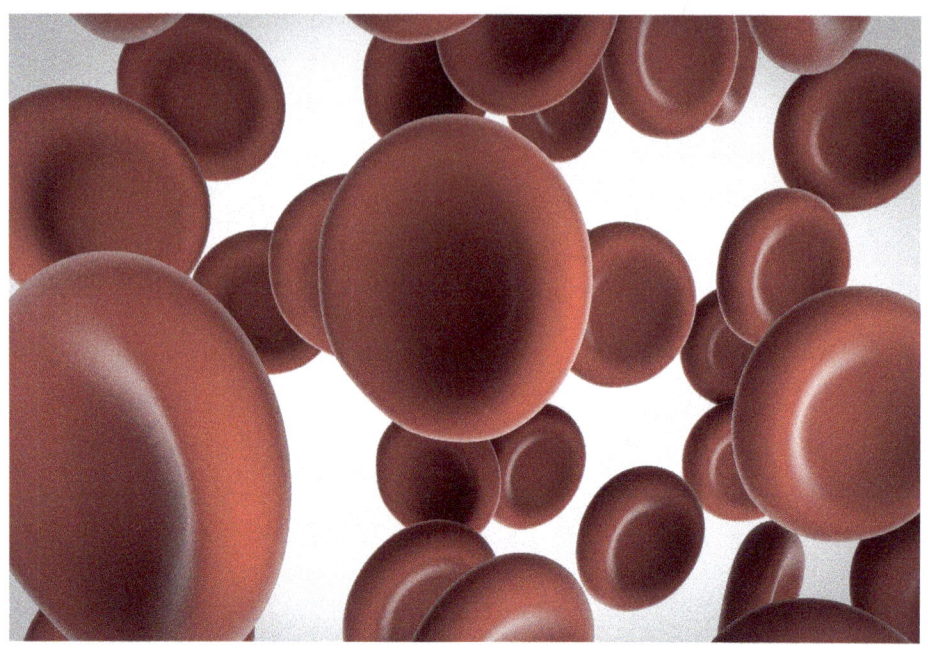

Fact# 16

The adult human body contains about 5.6 liters of blood.

The average adult human body contains around 5 to 6 quarts, which is approximately equal to 4.7 to 5.6 litres of blood. Blood is a crucial fluid that moves throughout the body, carrying vital substances such as oxygen and nutrients to cells and removing waste products for elimination. It also performs an essential role in maintaining body temperature and overall homeostasis. The amount of blood in a human body may vary slightly depending on factors such as age, sex, weight, and overall health. However, the estimated range of 5 to 6 quarts gives a general idea of the typical blood volume in an adult human body.

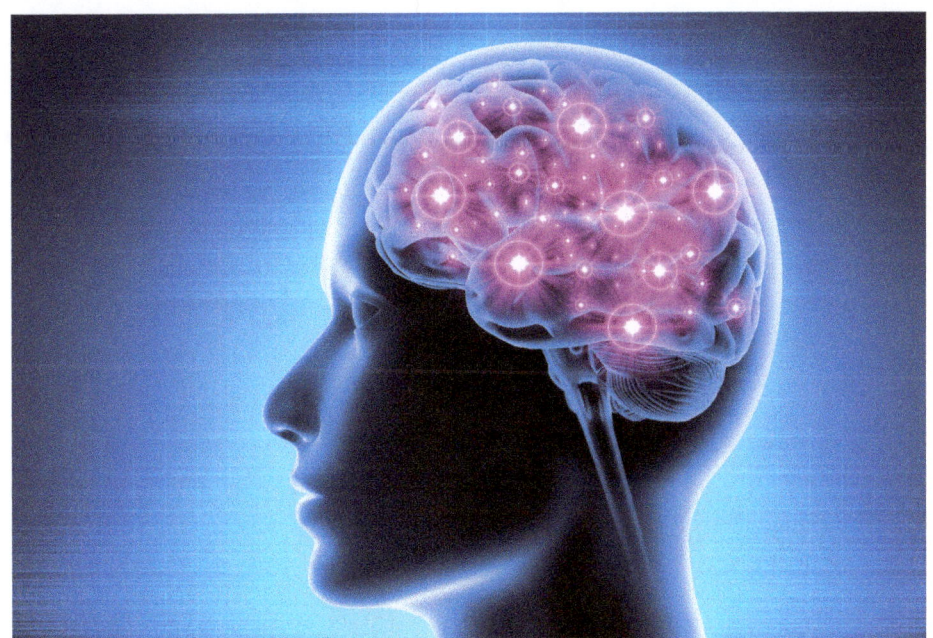

Fact# 17

Did you know that our brain doesn't feel pain at all?

The brain itself does not feel pain because it lacks pain receptors, also known as nociceptors. Nociceptors are specialized sensory nerve endings that detect and transmit the sensation of pain from various parts of the body to the brain. Although the brain is a vital organ that controls and processes pain signals from the rest of the body, it does not possess the ability to sense pain within itself. This is why neurosurgeons can perform brain surgeries on awake patients, as long as the anaesthesia is applied to the surrounding tissues, not the brain itself. While the brain can process and interpret pain signals from other body parts, it cannot experience pain directly.

Fact# 18

Did you know that you are actually taller in the morning than in the evening?

It is a common phenomenon that most people are slightly taller in the morning than in the evening. This is because the spinal discs compress and decompress throughout the day. During the night, when you are asleep, your spinal discs relax and decompress, allowing them to absorb fluid and expand. As a result, you tend to wake up slightly taller in the morning. However, as you go about your daily activities, such as standing, sitting, and walking, the force of gravity and physical stresses cause the spinal discs to gradually lose some of the fluid they absorb during the night. This leads to a slight reduction in height by the end of the day. The height difference is usually minimal, usually just a few millimetres. This change in height is a normal and temporary variation caused by the dynamic nature of the spine and the intervertebral discs.

Fact# 19

Did you know that human hair can sprout up to 6 inches every year?

Hair growth is a fascinating and variable process that varies among individuals. It can lead to hair lengthening up to 6 inches in a year. On average, human hair grows at a rate of about half an inch (or 1.25 centimetres) each month, but it can vary due to genetics, age, health, and diet. Hair growth is not a constant process and occurs in cycles. Whether hair is growing rapidly or gradually, it remains one of the most visible and versatile features of human appearance, serving as a protective and insulating element and a form of self-expression. Maintaining healthy hair requires proper care of the hair and scalp, balanced nutrition, and addressing underlying health concerns.

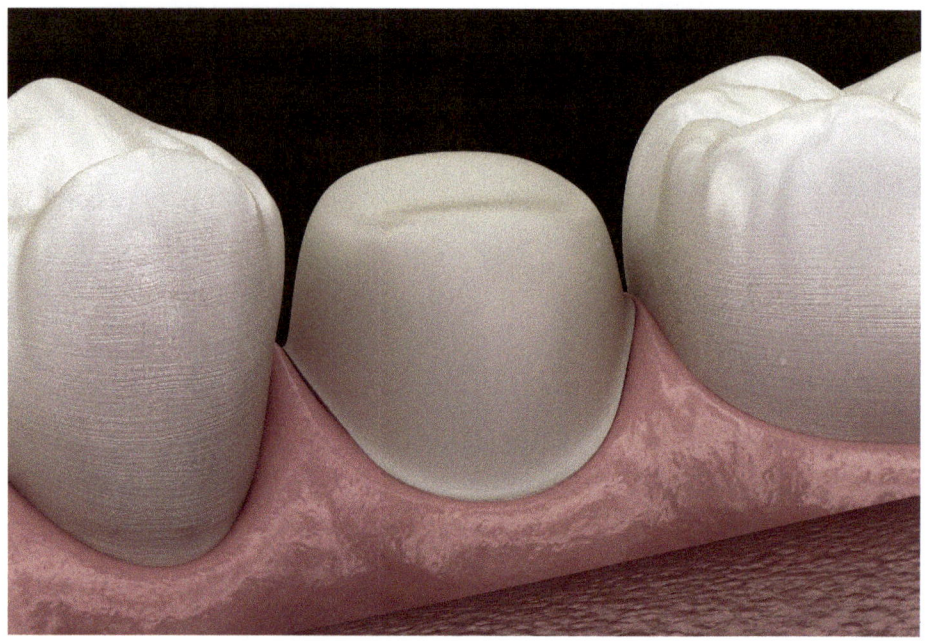

Fact# 20

Did you know that the hardest substance in your body is not your bones, but rather the enamel that covers your teeth?

The tooth enamel is mainly made of hydroxyapatite, a crystalline structure composed of calcium and phosphate. This mineralized tissue is incredibly hard and robust, protecting the underlying dentin and pulp of the tooth. Enamel is even tougher than bone and is highly resilient against wear and tear. However, it's not entirely immune to damage. Acid can erode it, physical trauma can chip or crack it, and dental decay or cavities can harm it. Therefore, it's essential to maintain good dental hygiene practices and dental care to preserve the enamel's integrity and maintain excellent oral health.

Fact# 21

The human body has a unique scent that dogs can identify.

Each person has a distinct and specific scent, often referred to as a "scent fingerprint." This unique scent arises from a combination of various chemical compounds our bodies produce, including those released through sweat and natural skin oils. Humans constantly emit a subtle aroma, which is made up of chemical compounds found in sweat, skin oils, and other bodily secretions. Dogs, with their highly developed sense of smell, have the incredible ability to detect and differentiate between these individual human scents. It is one of the reasons why they can be so skilled at tracking and recognizing familiar people.

Fact# 22

A human heart can continue to beat even after it has been removed from the body.

Under specific conditions in a medical setting, the human heart can continue to beat outside the body. In situations like open-heart surgery or heart transplant procedures, the heart can be temporarily supported using artificial devices, such as heart-lung machines or mechanical heart pumps. During these procedures, the heart may be stopped, and an artificial device takes over the heart's pumping function. This allows surgeons to work on the heart while maintaining oxygenated blood flow to the rest of the body. Once the surgical procedure is complete, the heart can be restarted. In the case of a heart transplant, the donor's heart starts beating outside the body before it is transplanted into the recipient and connected to the circulatory system.

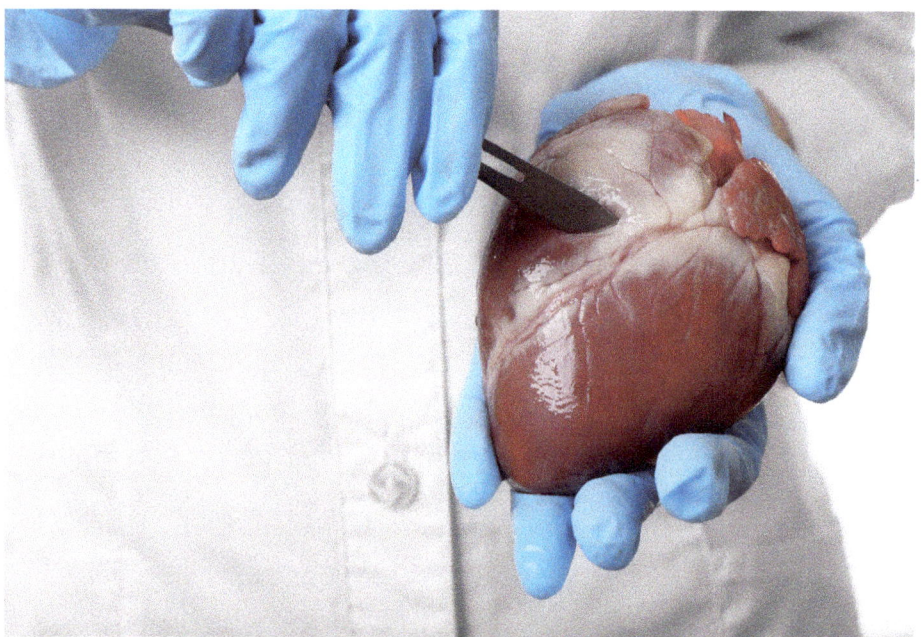

Fact# 23

Fun Fact: It's impossible to swallow and breathe in at the same time!

The act of swallowing involves a complex series of coordinated movements in the throat and oesophagus, temporarily closing the airway to prevent food or liquid from entering the lungs. This protects the respiratory system from choking and aspiration of foreign material into the lungs. When you swallow, a small flap of tissue called the epiglottis covers the trachea (the windpipe) to prevent food and liquids from entering the airway. This process ensures that the food or drink travels down the oesophagus and into the stomach rather than the respiratory system. So, in order to swallow, you must briefly stop breathing to allow the swallowing reflex to occur. Once the swallowing process is complete, normal breathing resumes.

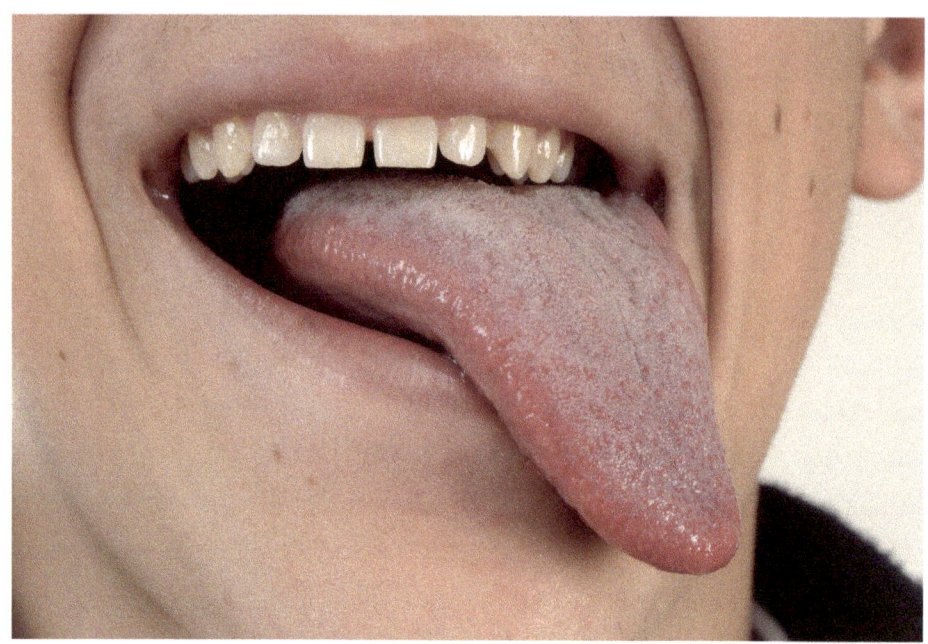

Fact# 24

Did you know? Just like fingerprints, humans also possess a unique tongue print.

While fingerprints are one of the most commonly used biometric identifiers, the uniqueness of the tongue's surface is also recognized in the field of biometrics. The specific patterns of papillae, taste buds, and other features on the tongue make it distinctive for each individual. However, using tongue prints for identification is less common and widespread than fingerprints or other biometric methods like iris scans or facial recognition. Fingerprints are preferred for their practicality and accuracy. Researchers have explored the idea of using tongue prints for identification and authentication in specific specialized applications.

Fact# 25

Have you ever wondered why farts have a bad smell?

The unpleasant odour associated with flatulence (fart) is primarily due to the presence of gases produced by bacteria in the gastrointestinal tract. When you digest food, various gases are produced as a natural byproduct of the digestive process. These gases include hydrogen, methane, and carbon dioxide. While these gases are odourless, the characteristic smell of a fart comes from small amounts of sulfur-containing compounds, such as hydrogen sulfide and methyl mercaptan, that are also released. The production of these foul-smelling compounds is related to the fermentation of undigested food by bacteria in the colon. These bacteria break down complex carbohydrates and other substances, releasing gases and sulfur compounds.

Fact# 26

Human blood appears red due to the presence of iron in the blood.

Iron is the part of the haemoglobin molecule found in red blood cells. Hemoglobin is vital in carrying oxygen from the lungs to different tissues and organs throughout the body. When haemoglobin combines with oxygen in the lungs, it forms oxyhemoglobin, which is bright red. The heart then pumps this oxygenated blood to supply oxygen to the body's cells. Deoxygenated blood, which has released its oxygen to the body's tissues, appears darker in colour and can range from deep red to purplish, depending on the circumstances. The colour of blood is determined by the way light interacts with the oxygen-bound haemoglobin in red blood cells.

Fact# 27

Did you know that your knee joint is the largest joint in your body?

The knee joint is indeed the largest joint in the human body. The knee joint is crucial in enabling various movements and supporting the body's weight. It is made up of the femur (thigh bone), tibia (shin bone), and patella (kneecap), which allow for flexion and extension, as well as limited rotation of the leg. This complex joint is responsible for facilitating activities such as walking, running, jumping, and various lower-body movements. Due to its size and function, it plays an essential role in our musculoskeletal system, making it a central player in our daily activities and mobility.

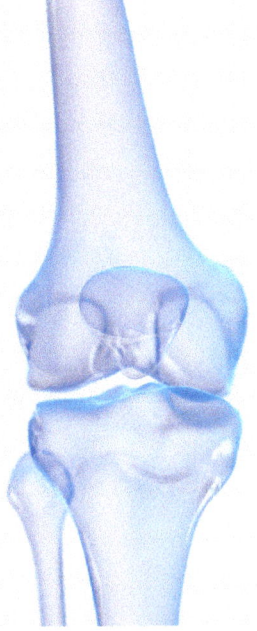
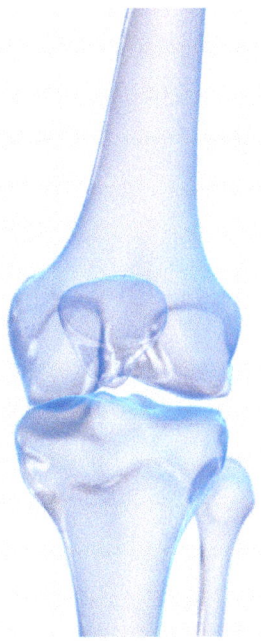

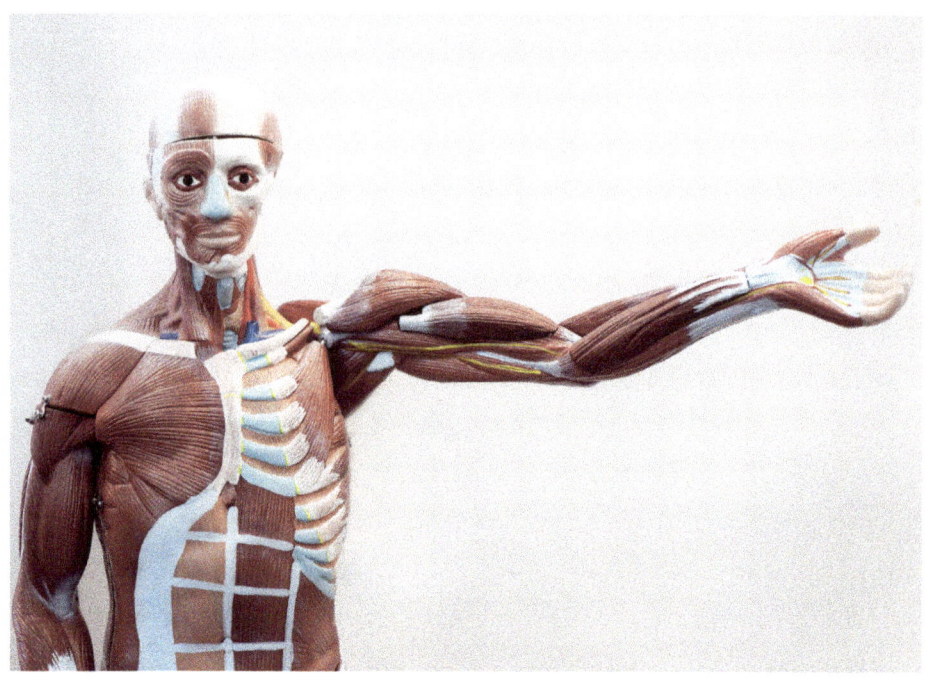

Fact# 28

The human body contains more than 600 muscles.

These muscles come in various sizes and shapes and serve a wide range of functions, from enabling voluntary movements like walking and lifting to controlling involuntary processes such as heart beating and food digestion. Muscles are grouped into different categories, including skeletal muscles (responsible for voluntary movements), smooth muscles (found in organs like the digestive tract), and cardiac muscles (which make up the heart). This vast array of muscles collectively allows us to perform diverse activities and maintain our overall health and functionality.

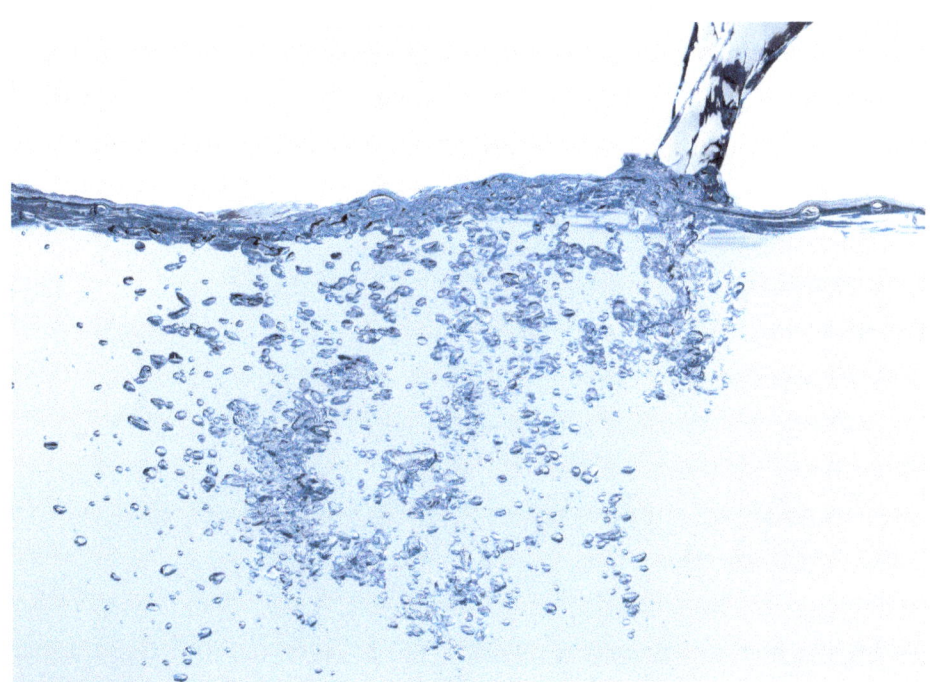

Fact# 29

Did you know that a majority of your body - around 60% - is actually made up of water?

Water is a vital human body component and plays a crucial role in various physiological processes. It is present in cells, tissues, and organs, regulates body temperature, transports nutrients and oxygen, removes waste products, and maintains overall health. Although the exact percentage of water in the body varies from person to person due to factors like age, sex, and body composition, a rough estimate of 60% is a commonly cited figure. Properly hydrating oneself is crucial to maintaining good health and ensuring that all bodily functions occur efficiently.

Fact# 30

Believe it or not, our bodies emit light, making us glow in the dark!

It is a fact that the human body emits a faint amount of visible light, although it is not detectable by the human eye. This natural process, known as bioluminescence, is caused by the metabolic processes within living cells. Bioluminescence is the production and emission of light by living organisms. In the case of the human body, this faint glow results from the chemical reactions and energy metabolism that occur in cells, particularly in the mitochondria. However, the amount of light emitted by the human body is extremely small and is overwhelmed by the ambient light in our surroundings. This makes it impossible to notice the glow with the naked eye, and it is not something that would make a person appear to glow in the dark.

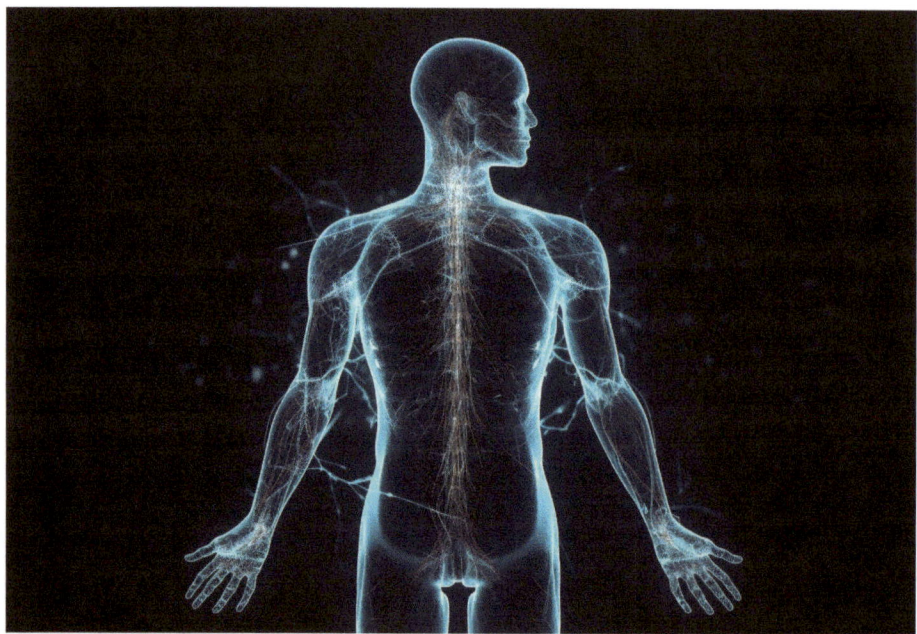

Fact# 31

Human brain may stay active for hours after death.

In general, when a person is declared clinically dead, it means that their vital signs, including heart rate and brain activity, have ceased. However, there have been some reported instances in which certain metabolic and electrical processes in the brain continue for a short period after clinical death. This phenomenon is sometimes referred to as "post-mortem" or "after-death" activity. Some research suggests that brain cells may remain active briefly after the cessation of circulation and oxygen supply, which can occur during the dying process. However, this activity is generally short-lived and rapidly declines. It is also important to note that this topic is still a subject of ongoing scientific investigation and debate.

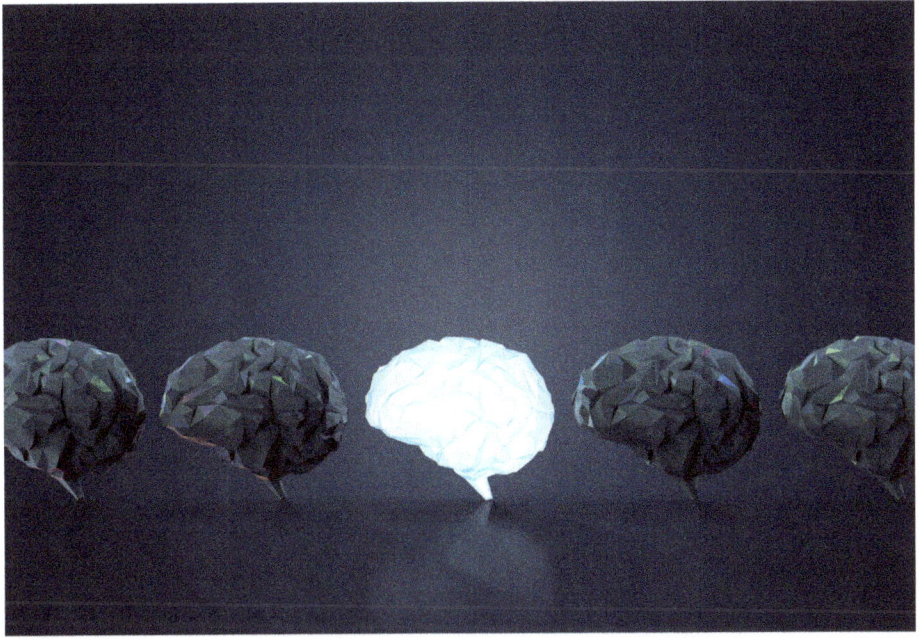

Fact# 32

Human sweat itself doesn't have a bad odour.

Sweat itself is usually odourless. However, it can develop an unpleasant odour when it comes into contact with bacteria on the skin's surface. Human sweat is composed primarily of water but contains small amounts of minerals and compounds, including salts, urea, and amino acids. When you sweat, these components can create an environment that encourages the growth of bacteria, particularly in areas where sweat tends to accumulate, such as the underarms and groin. The bacteria on the skin break down the sweat components, producing byproducts that can lead to body odour. This is why sweat can have an unpleasant smell. The specific odour can vary from person to person and can be influenced by factors like diet, hygiene, and genetics.

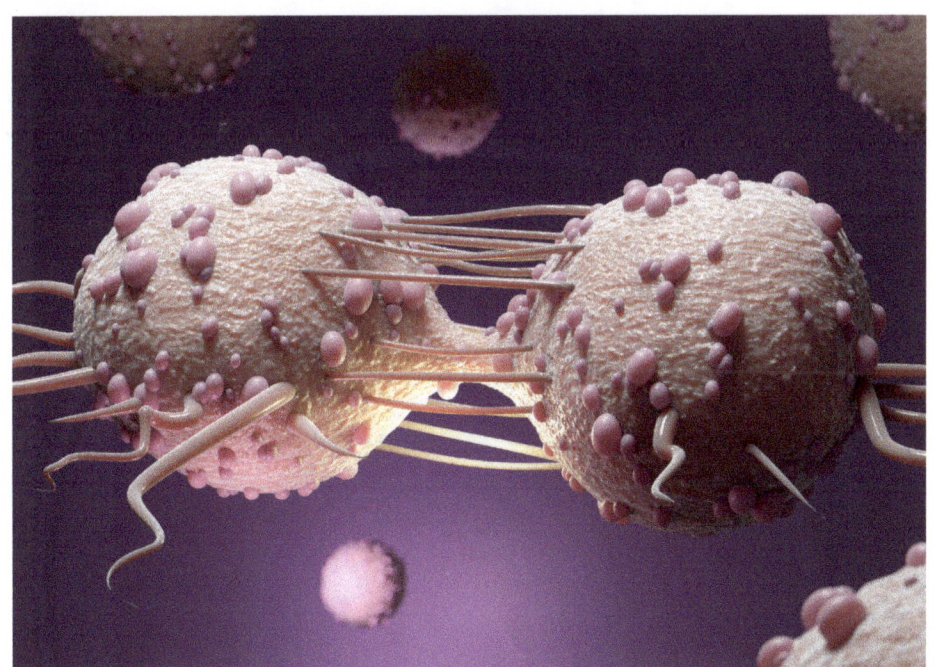

Fact# 33

Believe it or not, certain tumors, called teratomas, can sprout hair and even teeth!

Teratomas are a type of tumour that can contain various types of tissues, including hair, teeth, bone, and sometimes even organs. These tumours are typically composed of germ cells responsible for producing eggs and sperm. In rare cases, these germ cells can develop abnormally, giving rise to teratomas. Although teratomas are usually benign, meaning they are not cancerous, they can occasionally become malignant and spread to other body parts. Teratomas can appear in different body parts, most commonly in the ovaries, testes, and sacrococcygeal region (near the base of the spine). However, they can occasionally appear in other locations as well.

Fact# 34

Did you know that the eye is the fastest muscle in the human body?

The human eye can move incredibly swiftly, with some eye movements reaching speeds of up to 500 degrees per second. This incredible speed enables us to process visual information so rapidly, allowing us to take in the world around us with astounding efficiency. This is also why we say things happen "in the blink of an eye." The complexity and intricacy of the human body are evident in this remarkable ability, serving as a powerful reminder of our immense capabilities.

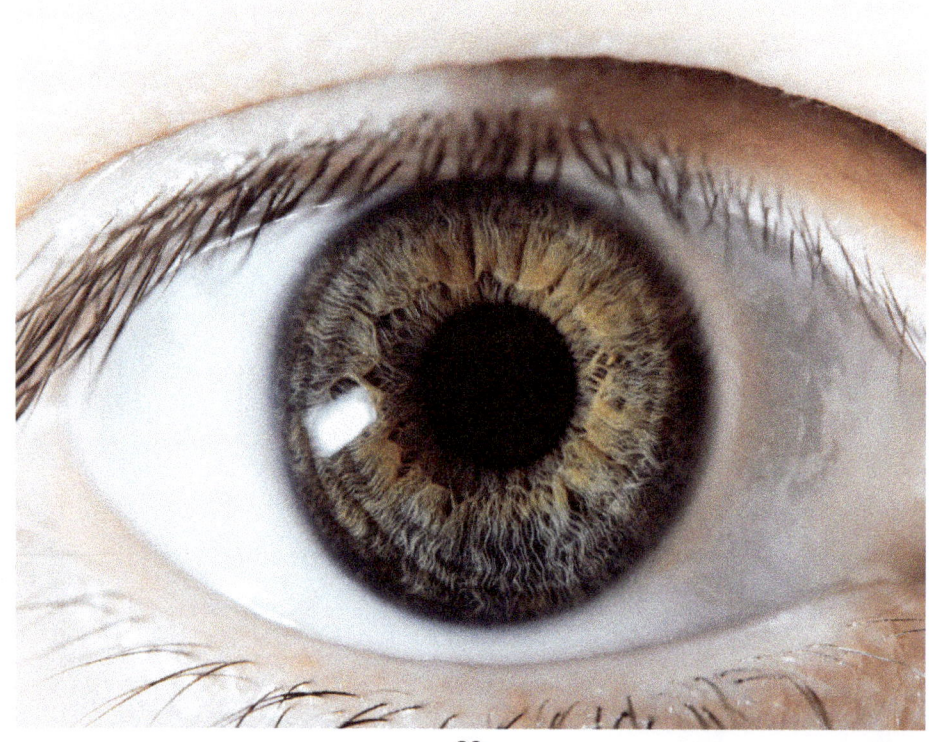

Fact# 35

Did you know that human ears keep growing throughout their entire life? Yes, It's true!

Unlike many other parts of our bodies that reach a point of maturity and remain static, our ears continue a subtle yet ceaseless expansion. This captivating phenomenon is attributed to the ongoing growth of cartilage in the ears, which maintains its vitality and flexibility over the years. The gradual enlargement of our ears might not be as conspicuous as the rapid growth experienced during adolescence, yet it's a silent and persistent process. Over the decades, the cartilage at the base of the ear elongates and thickens, contributing to the perceptible increase in size. While the growth rate is relatively slow and imperceptible in the short term, the cumulative effect becomes more apparent as the years pass.

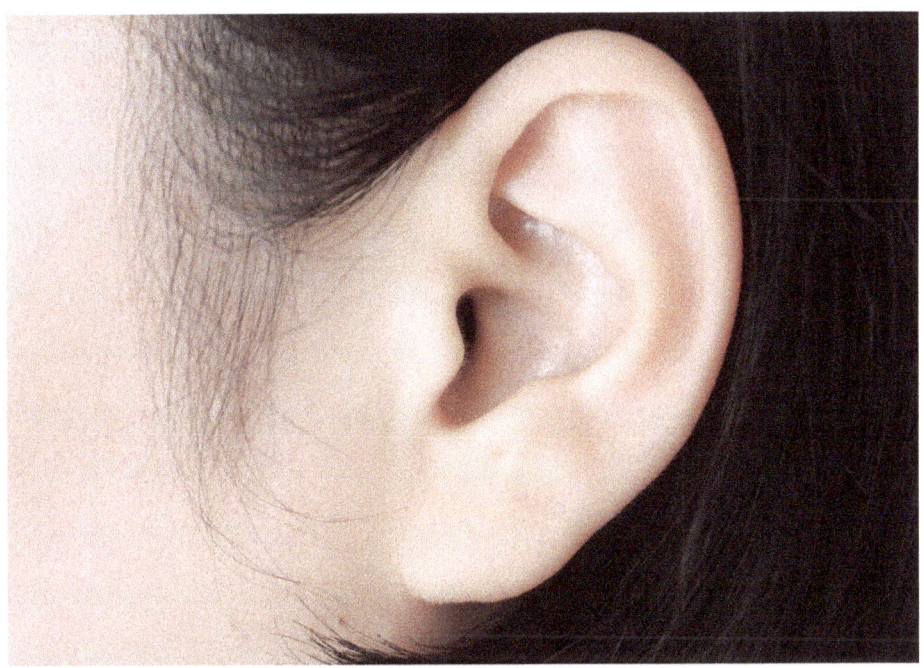

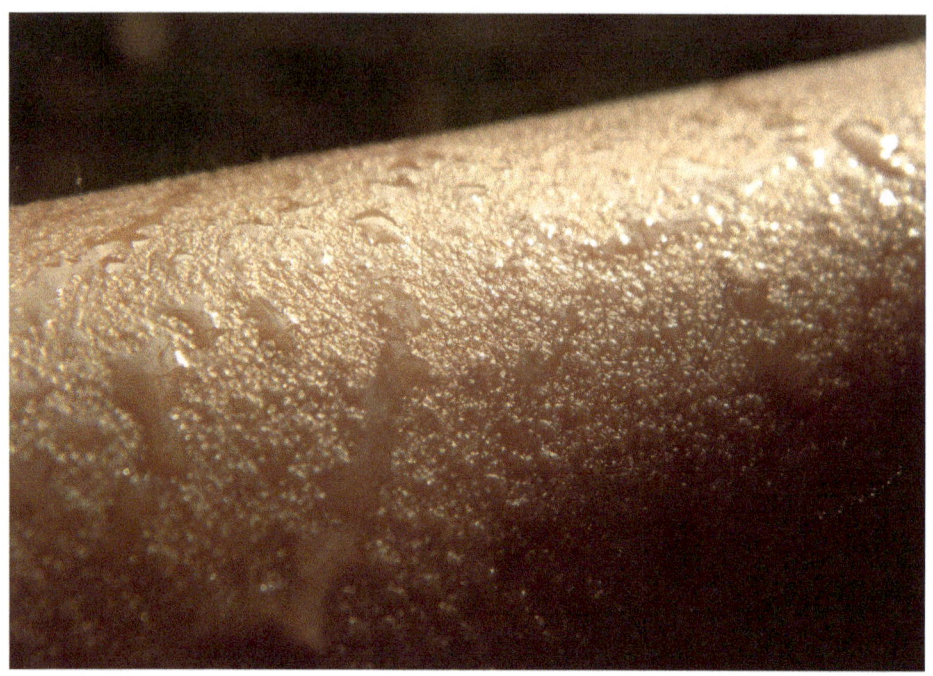

Fact# 36

Did you know that there are approximately 2 to 5 million sweat glands in the human body?

The vast number of sweat glands present in our body is truly remarkable, showcasing the incredible evolutionary design of our biology. Each gland is located beneath the surface of our skin and works like a miniature factory that produces sweat - an essential mechanism that helps in regulating our body temperature. During physical exertion or exposure to high temperatures, these glands work tirelessly to create sweat, which cools down the body when it evaporates. This incredible network of sweat glands functions continuously, responding to internal and external cues to maintain the perfect balance of our internal temperature.

Fact# 37

The stomach acid is so strong that it can dissolve certain metals.

The human stomach contains hydrochloric acid, a very strong acid that helps break down food. This acid has a pH level of 1 to 2, which means it is highly acidic and can dissolve many materials, including some metals. However, it should be noted that the acid can only dissolve certain metals, such as zinc and aluminium, and not all metals. Additionally, the acid is typically not strong enough to damage metal objects swallowed accidentally. Despite its remarkable ability to dissolve certain metals, stomach acid plays a crucial role in digestion.

Fact# 38

Did you know that your fingernails actually grow 3 times faster than your toenails?

The rate at which nails grow can vary depending on various factors such as age, gender, diet, and overall health. However, fingernails grow at about 3 millimetres per month, while toenails grow at about 1 millimetre per month. This means that fingernails can grow three times faster than toenails. This difference in growth rate may be due to differences in blood flow and the amount of keratin (a protein that makes nails) in the fingers and toes. Additionally, the pressure and friction that the toenails experience from walking and wearing shoes may also contribute to slower growth. Regardless of the reason, it's interesting to note that our nails can grow at different rates depending on where they are in our bodies.

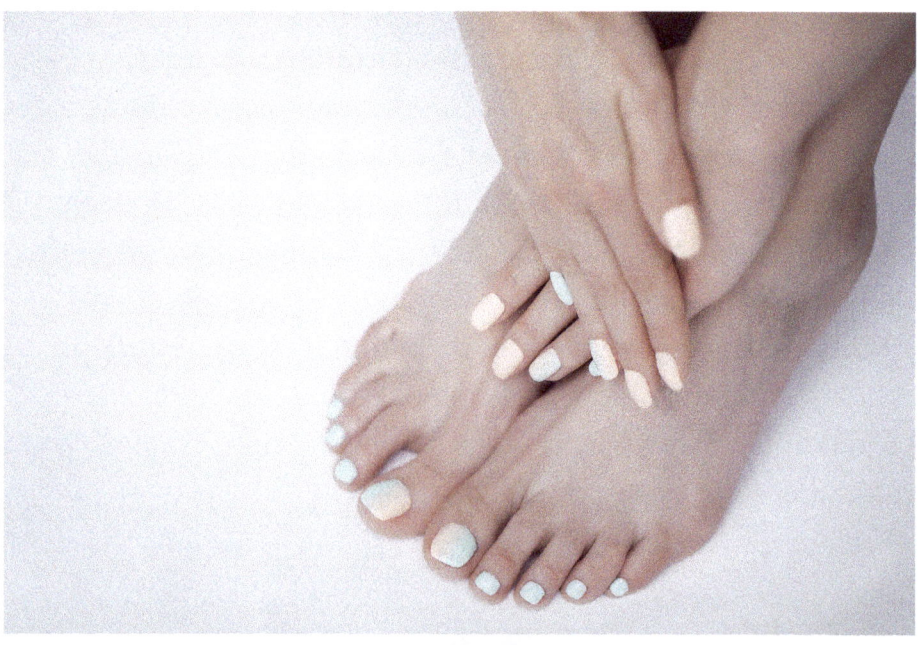

Fact# 39

People who dream vividly and frequently tend to have higher IQs.

Several studies have found a correlation between high IQ and frequent, vivid dreams. One theory is that dreaming is linked to the brain's ability to process and store information. People with high IQs may have more active brains, leading to more vivid and complex dreams. Additionally, some research has suggested that more creative people have more vivid and frequent dreams, and creativity and intelligence often go hand in hand. However, it's important to note that correlation does not necessarily mean causation and more research is needed to fully understand the relationship between dreaming, creativity, and intelligence.

Fact# 40

There's a word for the fear of being ignored or forgotten. It's called Athazagoraphobia! Let's see if you can pronounce it!

People who experience this phobia often believe that they are insignificant and that they will be left alone or abandoned by others. This fear can be triggered by various situations, such as when someone doesn't respond to their messages or is excluded from social events. Studies have found that people who dream more often and vividly are more likely to have this fear. Dreams often reflect our subconscious thoughts and fears and may reveal our deepest anxieties. Therefore, if someone is experiencing athazagoraphobia, their dreams may feature scenarios where they are being ignored or forgotten by others.

Fact# 41

Did you know that beards are the fastest-growing hairs on the human body?

Beards are a type of facial hair that grows on men's chin, cheeks, and neck. They are known to be the fastest-growing hairs on the human body, with an average growth rate of around half an inch per month. This is due to the presence of androgen hormones, which stimulate the growth of hair follicles in the face. Age, genetics, and overall health can affect the growth rate. Interestingly, the growth rate of beards tends to slow as men get older, with some experiencing patchy or thinning beards due to decreased hormone levels.

Fact# 42

Did you know the sound of joints cracking is caused by bubbles popping in the joint fluid?

We hear a distinct popping or cracking sound when we crack our knuckles, necks, backs, or other joints. This sound is caused by the sudden release of gas that has built up in the joint's synovial fluid. Synovial fluid is a thick, transparent liquid that lubricates and cushions the joints. It contains dissolved gases like oxygen, carbon dioxide, and nitrogen. When we stretch or bend a joint, the pressure inside the synovial fluid changes, causing some gas to come out of the solution and form bubbles. When these bubbles collapse or burst, they create a popping or cracking sound. The sound can be loud or soft, depending on how much gas and fast it is released. Although cracking your joints doesn't cause arthritis or severe health problems, but excessive cracking may lead to joint irritation or swelling over time.

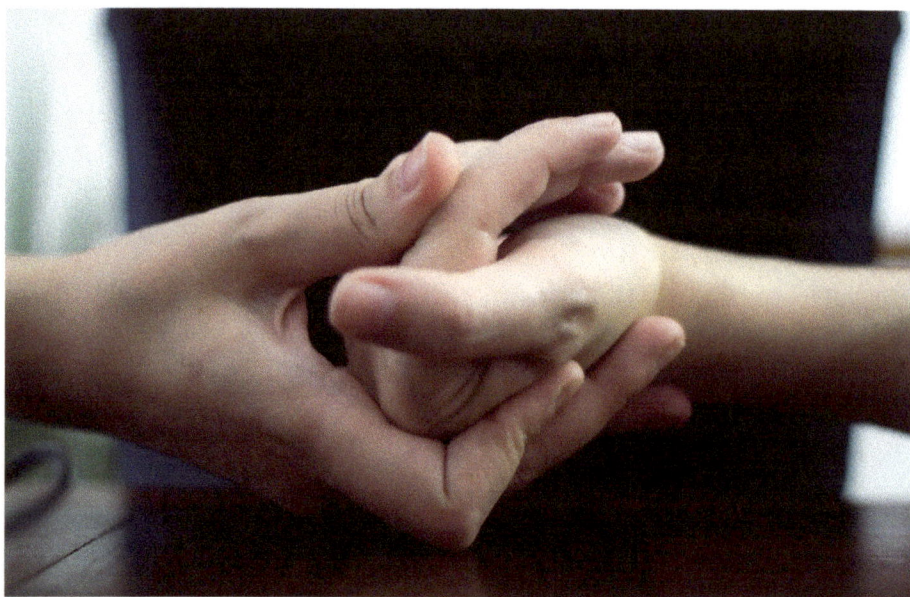

Fact# 43

Have you ever wondered how human skin colour is determined?

The colour of human skin is determined primarily by the presence and distribution of a pigment called melanin. Melanin is produced by melanocytes, cells in the skin's outermost layer, the epidermis. There are two primary types of melanin: eumelanin, responsible for brown and black pigments, and pheomelanin, which contributes to red and yellow pigments. The ratio and amount of these pigments and their distribution influence the various shades of skin colour among individuals. Darker skin is generally associated with higher levels of eumelanin, while lighter skin is associated with lower or more pheomelanin. An individual's skin colour is determined by both genetic and environmental factors, including sun exposure, which can stimulate melanin production.

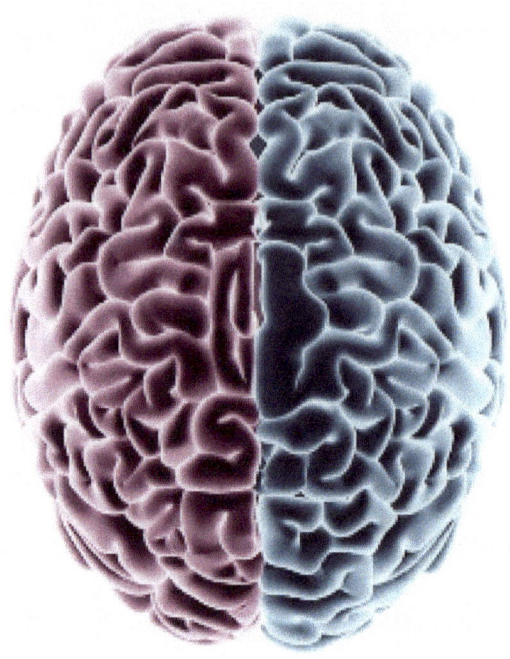

Fact# 44

Did you know the left brain controls the right side, and the right brain controls the left?

This phenomenon is known as contralateral control. The nervous system is divided into two hemispheres, the left and the right, and each hemisphere is responsible for controlling and processing information from the opposite side of the body. This is due to the crossing of nerve fibres, or decussation, in the brainstem. For example, the motor cortex on the left side of the brain controls voluntary movements on the right side of the body and vice versa. Similarly, sensory information from the right side of the body is processed in the left hemisphere, and sensory information from the left side is processed in the right hemisphere.

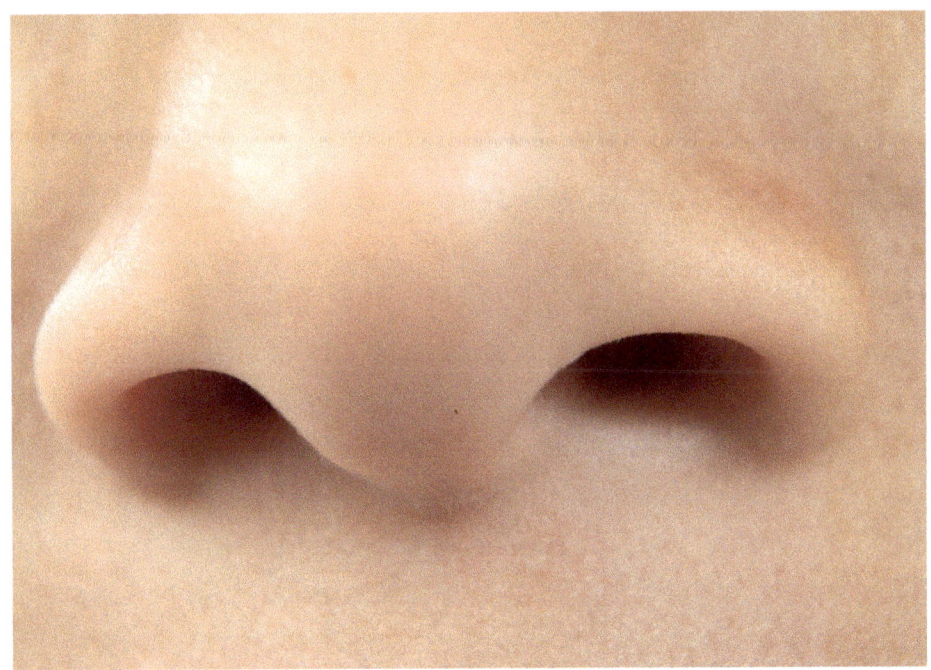

Fact# 45

Did you know that the hairs inside our nose serve a purpose?

The nose has tiny hair-like structures, known as cilia, present in the nasal passages. These cilia are essential for the respiratory system as they help to clean and filter the air we breathe. As air enters the nasal passages, the cilia catch particles such as dust, pollen, bacteria, and other foreign particles. The cilia move in coordinated waves, sweeping the trapped particles towards the back of the nose and into the throat. These particles can be swallowed or expelled from the body via coughing or sneezing. This mechanism is the first line of defence for the respiratory system and prevents harmful particles from reaching the lungs.

Fact# 46

The lungs are the only organs in the human body that can float on water.

The lungs are made up of tissues that are less dense than water, which is why they have the ability to float. This is due to the presence of air, which is lighter than water, in the tissues of the lungs. When a person takes a deep breath and holds it, the lungs become even more buoyant and can float on water. However, it is important to note that while the lungs can float on water, it is not a guaranteed sign of life. In drowning cases, the lungs may still contain air and float, even if the person has died.

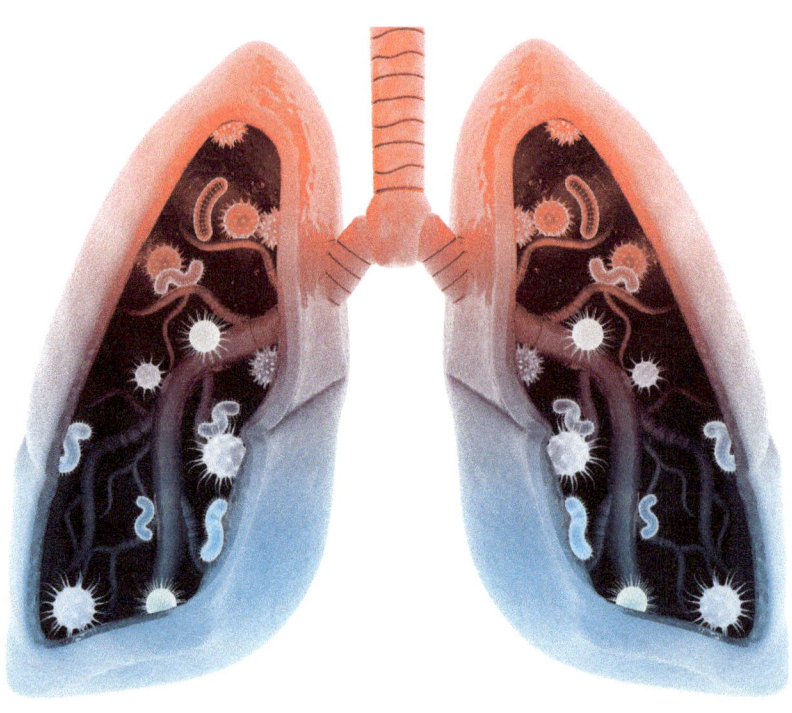

Fact# 47

Our digestive system can move food through our body even when we're asleep or upside down.

When we eat, food travels down our oesophagus and enters our stomach. From there, it passes through the small intestine, where nutrients are absorbed into the bloodstream. The remaining waste material then moves into the large intestine, where water is absorbed, and the waste material is prepared for elimination. The movement of food through our digestive system is controlled by muscles in the walls of the digestive tract, which contract and relax in a coordinated manner. These contractions, known as peristalsis, help to move the food along and break it down into smaller particles that can be absorbed.

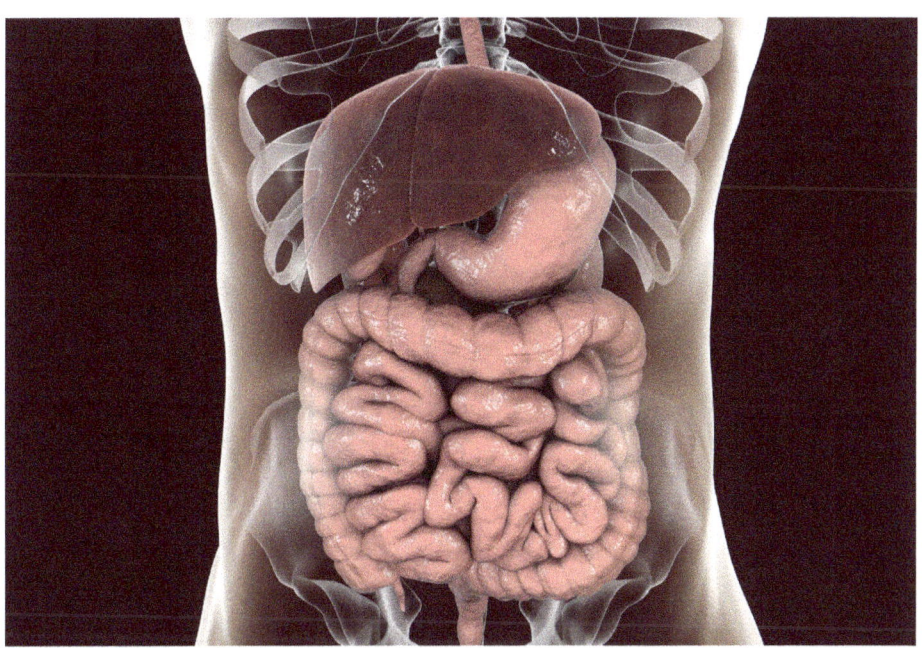

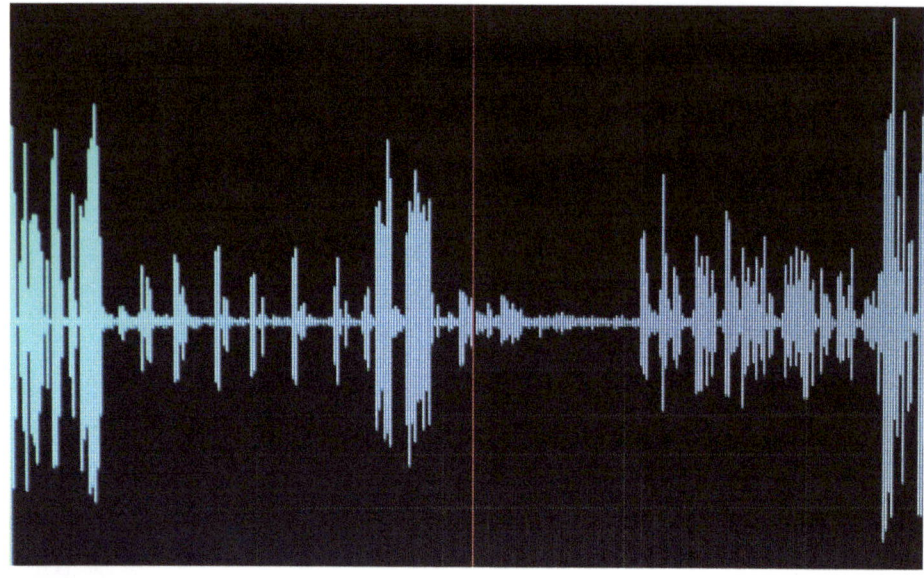

Fact# 48

The human ear can detect sounds up to 20 kHz.

The human ear is a complex organ capable of detecting a wide range of sounds. Sounds are vibrations that travel through the air in waves. The frequency of a sound wave determines its pitch, with higher frequencies producing higher-pitched sounds. The human ear can detect sounds with frequencies ranging from 20 Hz to 20 kHz. This range is known as the audible frequency range. Sounds with frequencies below 20 Hz are called infrasound, while those above 20 kHz are called ultrasound. The upper limit of the audible frequency range can vary from person to person depending on age, exposure to loud noises, and other factors. Overall, the fact that humans can hear sounds up to 20 kHz is a testament to the human ear's remarkable capabilities and the auditory system's intricacies.

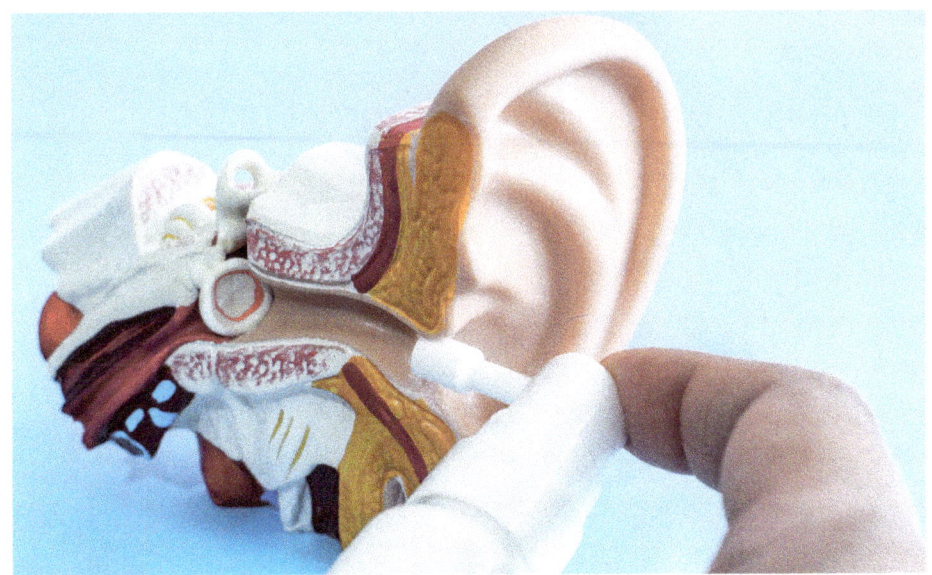

Fact# 49

Can you believe it? Earwax is not just some random substance but a type of sweat!

Earwax, also known as cerumen, is a waxy substance that is secreted by glands in the skin of the ear canal. It is made up of a combination of sweat, dead skin cells, and oil. The sweat glands in the ear canal produce a special type of sweat known as apocrine sweat, which is high in fats and proteins. This sweat combines with the dead skin cells and oil to form earwax. The function of earwax is to protect the ear canal from dirt, dust, and other foreign particles. It also helps lubricate the ear canal's skin, preventing it from drying out and becoming itchy. So, in summary, earwax is not just some random substance but a combination of sweat, dead skin cells, and oil that serves an important purpose in protecting and lubricating the ear canal.

Fact# 50

There is a popular myth that suggests humans only use 10% of their brains, but this is not true.

The idea that humans only use 10% of their brains is a common myth that has been perpetuated in popular culture. The truth is that our brains are constantly active, and we use much more than 10% of its capacity on a regular basis. Every part of the brain has a specific function, and different brain regions are responsible for different tasks, such as controlling movement, processing sensory information, and regulating emotions. While it is true that there may be some unused or underutilized areas of the brain, the idea that we only use 10% of our brain is not accurate. Our brains are incredibly complex and powerful organs that are constantly working to help us navigate the world around us.

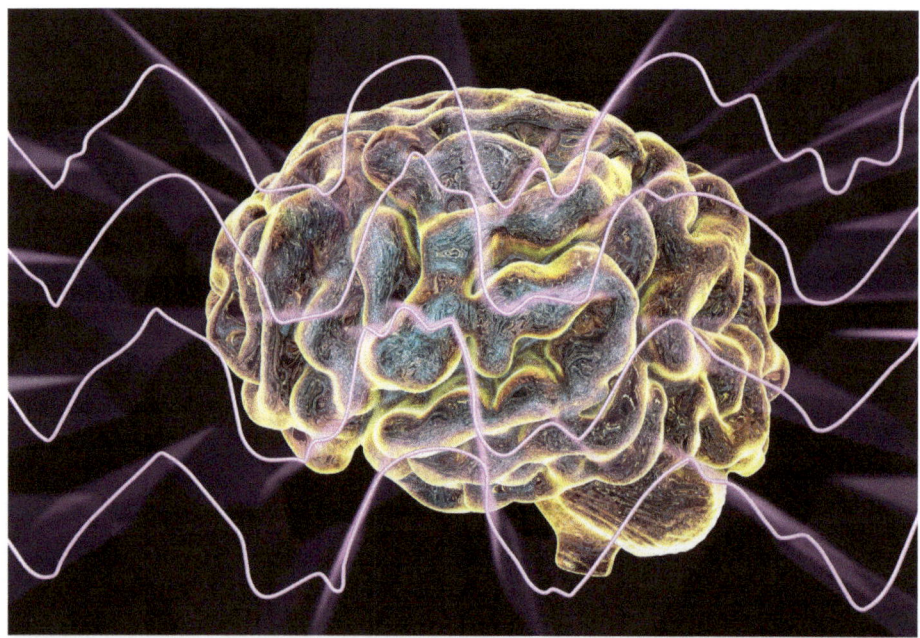

Fact# 51

The human tongue is covered with approximately 8,000 taste buds.

The tongue helps us taste and swallow food. The tongue's surface is covered in thousands of small bumps called papillae containing taste buds. Taste buds are clusters of cells with specialized receptors for detecting different types of taste, such as sweet, sour, salty, bitter, and umami. On average, an adult human tongue has approximately 8,000 taste buds, although the number can vary from person to person. Interestingly, taste buds are located not just on the tongue's surface but also on the mouth's roof, the throat's back, and even on the epiglottis, a flap of tissue that prevents food from entering the windpipe during swallowing. The taste buds play an important role in our sense of taste, helping us to distinguish between different flavours and textures of food.

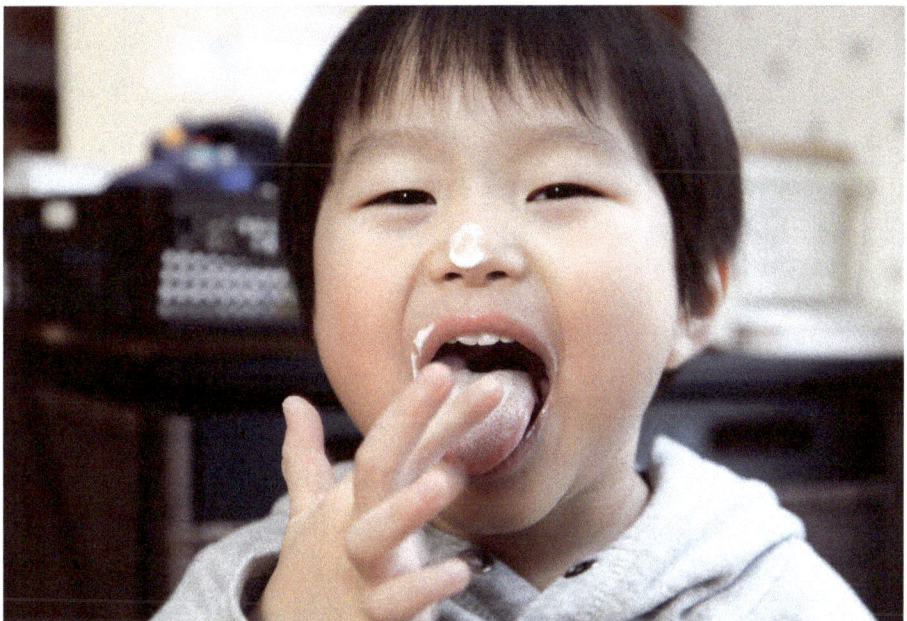

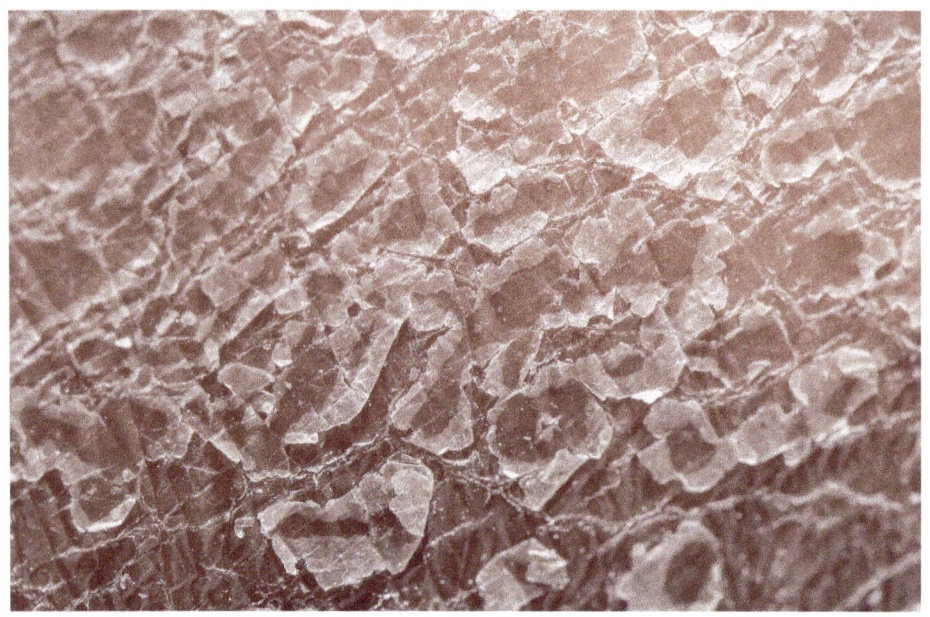

Fact# 52

Did you know? Every month, our skin gets a complete makeover! It's like we're shedding our old skin to reveal a new layer.

The process of skin regeneration is a continuous and complex cycle that occurs throughout our lives. Skin cells are constantly dividing and growing in the deeper layers of the skin, and as they mature, they move towards the surface, where they eventually die and are shed. This shedding process is known as desquamation. On average, it takes about a month for new skin cells to reach the surface and for old, dead skin cells to be shed. This means that every month, the outermost layer of our skin is completely replaced with a new layer of skin cells. This process helps keep our skin healthy, smooth, and damage-free. Factors such as age, genetics, and lifestyle habits can affect the rate of skin regeneration and can lead to changes in the appearance and health of our skin.

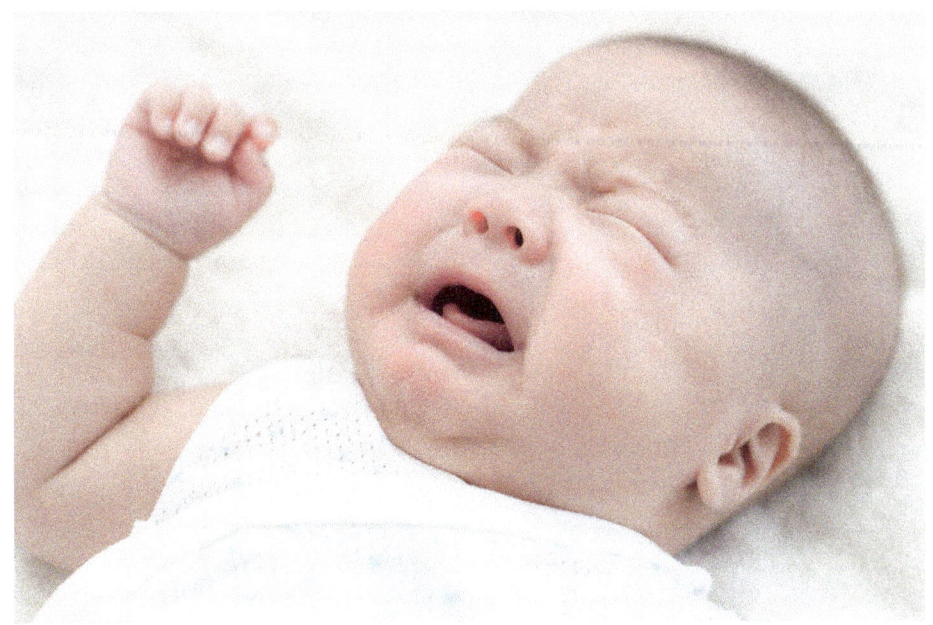

Fact# 53

Here's an interesting fact: Did you know that newborns don't cry tears until they hit their one-month mark?

Babies don't shed tears until they are at least one month old due to their underdeveloped tear ducts. Tear ducts are responsible for producing and draining tears, which help keep our eyes moist and free of irritants. In newborns, these ducts are not fully formed or open yet, so they cannot produce tears like adults. Instead, babies rely on other methods to clear their eyes, such as blinking or a small amount of moisture naturally present in the eye. It typically takes about 3-4 weeks for a baby's tear ducts to fully develop, after which they will start producing tears in response to various stimuli, such as pain, sadness, or irritation.

Fact# 54

Based on weight, the strongest muscle in our body is the masseter in the jaw.

The masseter muscle is a thick, rectangular-shaped muscle that occupies the cheekbone area and connects the lower jawbone (mandible) to the cheekbone (zygomatic bone). This muscle plays a crucial role in the process of chewing and biting food. It is the primary muscle responsible for the elevation of the mandible, which is the movement of the lower jawbone towards the upper jawbone (maxilla). The masseter muscle is considered the strongest muscle in the human body based on weight. It can generate a force of up to 600 pounds (272 kg) in the back teeth during biting. This strength is essential for the breakdown of food into smaller particles before swallowing and digestion can occur.

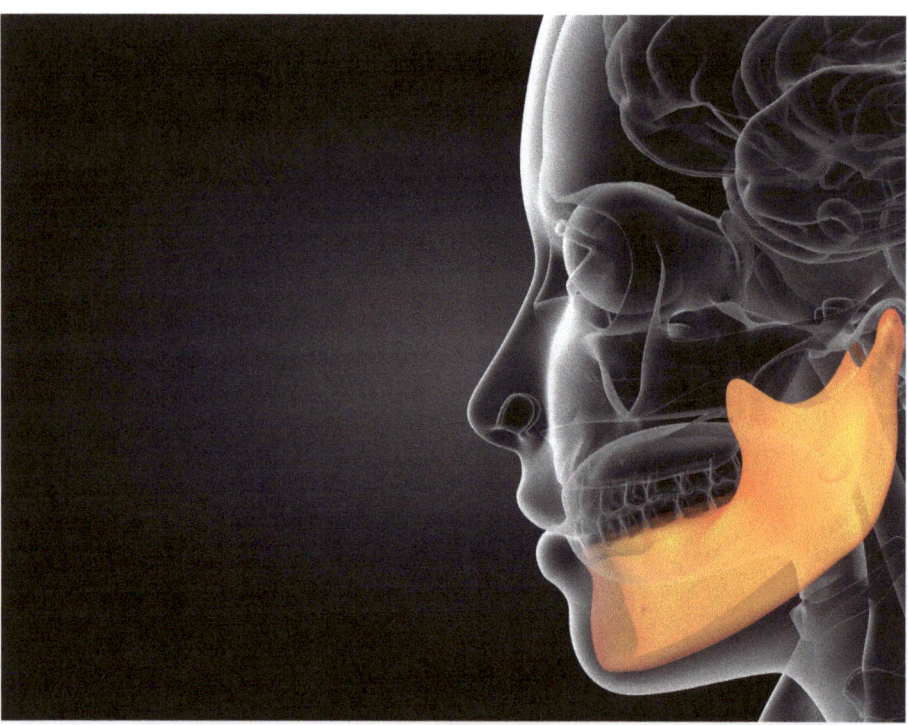

Fact# 55

Wisdom teeth, the final set of molars, have nothing to do with being wise!

Wisdom teeth, also known as third molars, are the last teeth to emerge in your mouth. They usually appear between ages 17 and 25, although some people may not get them at all. Wisdom teeth can cause problems if there is not enough space for them to grow properly. They may come in at an angle or only partially emerge, leading to pain, infection, and damage to adjacent teeth. In some cases, a dentist or oral surgeon may need to remove wisdom teeth to prevent further complications. It is important to have regular dental checkups to monitor the growth and development of your wisdom teeth and ensure they do not cause any problems in the future.

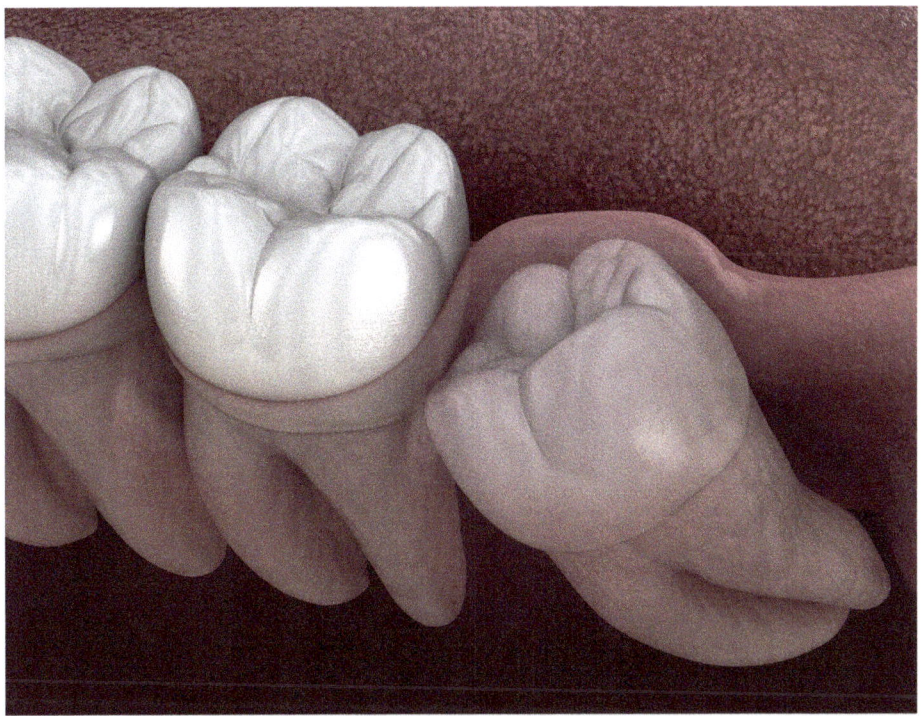

Fact# 56

When babies are born, they can only see in black and white.

As newborns enter the world, their eyes and visual systems are not fully developed. Their visual acuity is limited for the first few months, and they can only distinguish between high-contrast colours, such as black and white. As their visual system develops, they can gradually see colours and perceive more complex visual stimuli at around 4 months. This process is a crucial part of a baby's cognitive and sensory development, and it plays an essential role in their ability to interact with and understand the world around them. Moreover, parents and caregivers can aid in this process by providing babies with stimulating visual experiences, such as bright-coloured toys, to encourage their visual development.

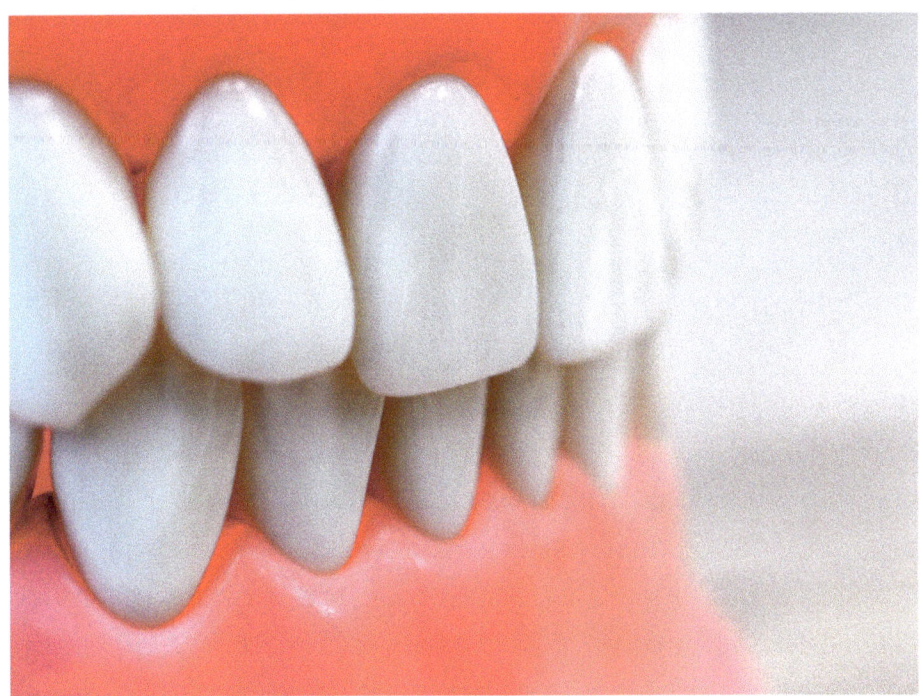

Fact# 57

Teeth are the only part of the human body that can not regenerate or heal themselves.

Unlike other body parts, such as the skin or bones, teeth cannot repair themselves once damaged or decayed. This is because teeth comprise a hard outer layer called enamel, a softer layer called dentin, and an inner layer called pulp, which contains nerves and blood vessels. While enamel is the hardest substance in the body, it is also brittle and can crack or chip easily. Once enamel is damaged, it cannot grow back or repair itself. Similarly, if the dentin or pulp is damaged, it can lead to tooth decay or infection, which can cause pain and ultimately result in tooth loss. Therefore, taking good care of your teeth by practising good oral hygiene and visiting the dentist regularly to prevent any potential damage or decay is essential.

Fact# 58

Your body generates enough heat in 30 minutes to boil half a gallon of water.

The human body constantly generates heat as a byproduct of its metabolic processes. This heat production is necessary for the body to maintain its core temperature and perform various physiological functions. According to scientific studies, the average human body generates enough heat in just half an hour to boil half a gallon of water. To put this into perspective, this amount of heat is equivalent to around 4000 joules of energy, roughly the same amount required to power a 100-watt light bulb for 40 minutes. This incredible heat production is evidence of the remarkable capabilities of the human body and its ability to perform and sustain various activities.

Fact# 59

There is a common misconception that hair and nails continue to grow after a person dies. However, this is not true.

What's actually happening is that after death, the body undergoes a series of physical changes as it begins to decompose. One of the most noticeable changes is the loss of moisture, which causes the skin to shrink and pull away from the nails and hair. This can give the appearance that the hair and nails have grown longer, but it is only an illusion. In reality, there is no biological process that allows hair and nails to continue to grow after death. The cells responsible for the growth of hair and nails require a steady supply of nutrients and oxygen, which are no longer available after the heart stops beating. As a result, the growth of hair and nails stops immediately after death.

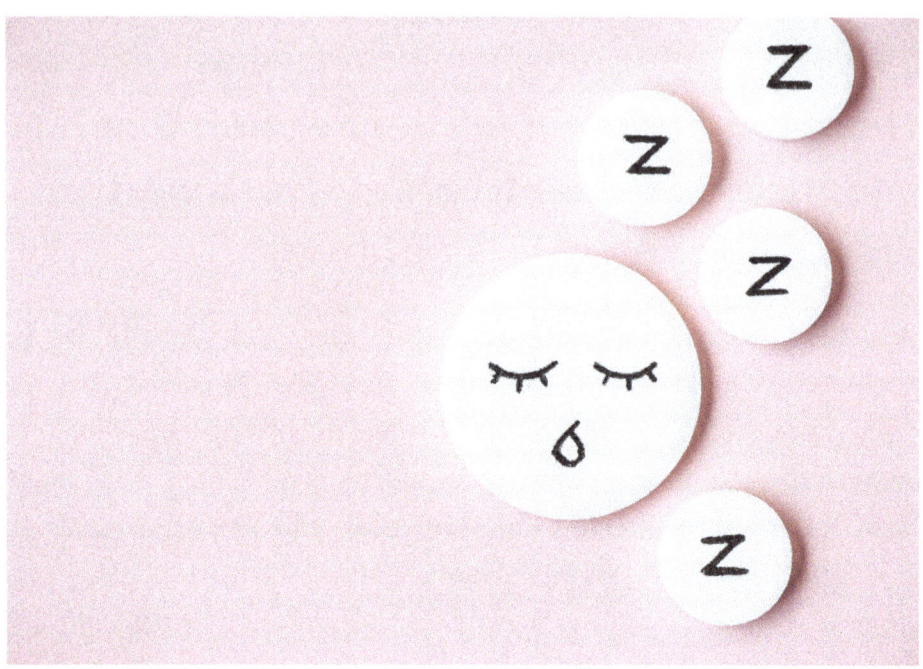

Fact# 60

Did you know that sleep is more crucial for humans than food? We can survive longer without food than without sleep.

The human body can survive for a longer period of time without food compared to sleep. This is because the body can use stored energy from fat and muscle tissues to sustain itself for a certain period of time without food. However, sleep is essential for the body to restore and repair itself. Lack of sleep can lead to various health problems, such as decreased cognitive function, lowered immunity, and increased risk of chronic diseases. While food is vital for providing energy and nutrients to the body, sleep is equally important for maintaining overall health and well-being.

Fact# 61

Did you know that it requires only 17 muscles to smile, but it takes 43 muscles to frown?

When you smile, the muscles around your mouth and eyes contract, but the rest of your face remains relaxed. This means that less energy is required to produce a smile compared to a frown, which involves the contraction of more muscles around the eyes, forehead and mouth. Frowning, however, is often associated with negative emotions, such as anger, sadness, and frustration, and can lead to increased stress and tension in the body. Overall, the fact that it takes fewer muscles to smile than to frown is a reminder that choosing a positive attitude over a negative one is often more accessible and beneficial. So, the next time you're feeling down, try smiling and see how it makes you feel!

Fact# 62

You cannot tickle yourself, no matter how hard you try!

The reason why it is impossible to tickle yourself is that your brain anticipates the sensation that comes from your own touch. This anticipation dampens the response that your brain would normally produce when someone else tickles you. In other words, your brain knows what to expect when you try to tickle yourself, so it doesn't send the same signals as if someone else were tickling. This is why you can't tickle yourself as effectively as someone else can. So, next time you try to tickle yourself, and it doesn't work, don't worry - it's just your brain doing its job!

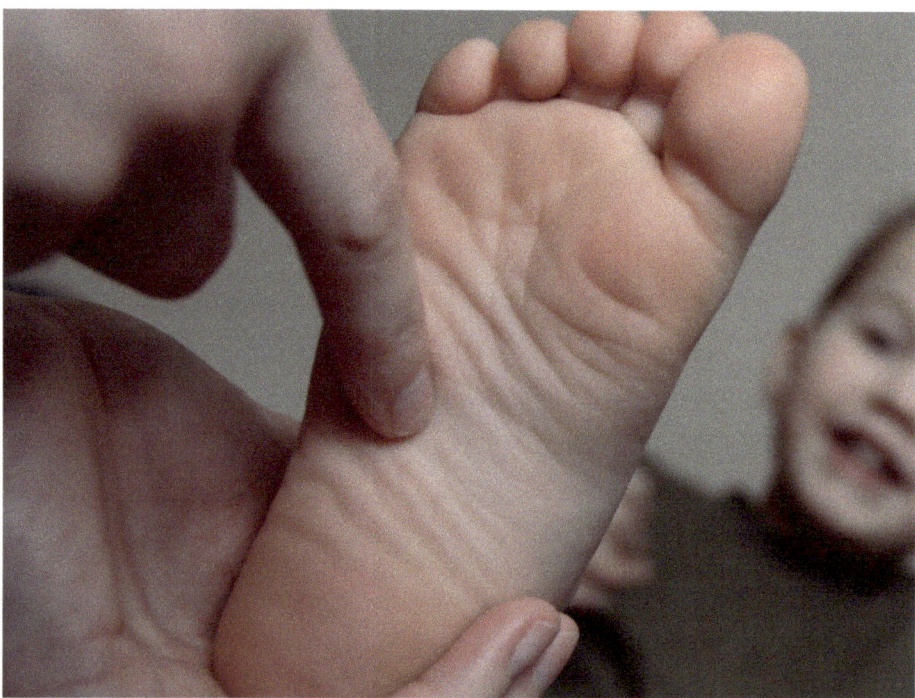

Fact# 63

Did you know that the feet hold one quarter of all the bones in the human body?

The human foot is an intricate structure comprising 26 bones each, 33 joints, and more than 100 muscles, tendons, and ligaments that work together to support the body's weight, balance, and movement. The feet carry the entire body's weight and absorb the shock of every step taken. It is fascinating to note that one-quarter of all the bones in the human body are located in the feet. The bones in the feet are designed to provide stability, flexibility, and mobility to the feet. The foot bones can be divided into three categories: the tarsals, metatarsals, and phalanges. The tarsal bones are the largest and strongest foot bones, while the phalanges form the toes.

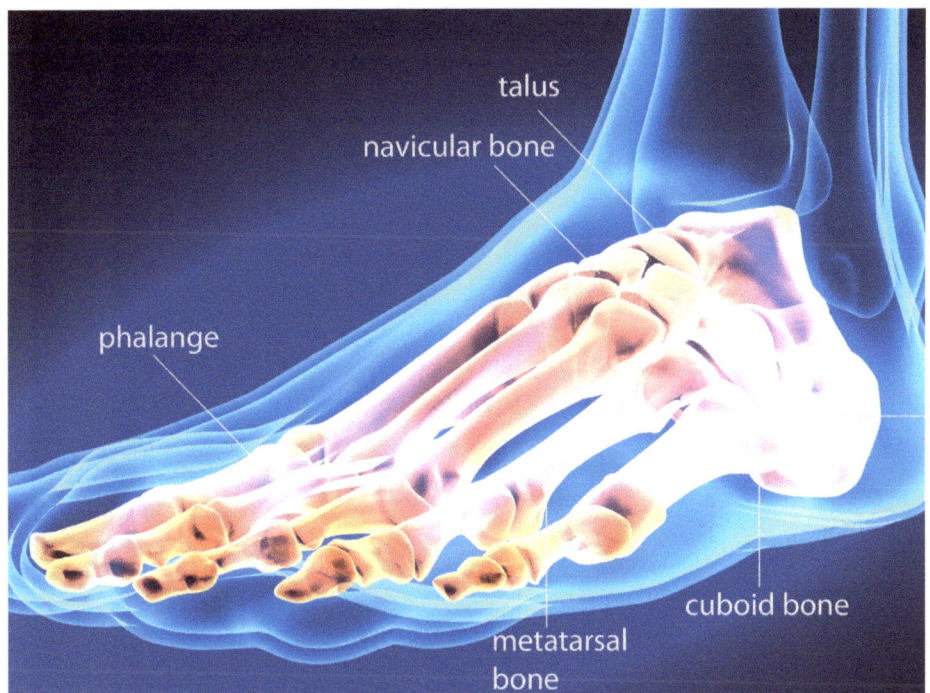

Fact# 64

Did you know that, on average, a person produces enough saliva to fill two bathtubs every year?

Saliva is a clear, watery liquid produced in the salivary glands and secreted into the mouth. The primary function of saliva is to aid in the digestion of food by moistening and lubricating it, making it easier to swallow. Saliva also contains enzymes that help break down carbohydrates, and it helps to neutralize acid in the mouth, which can help prevent tooth decay. On average, an adult produces between 0.5 and 1.5 litres of saliva per day, up to 182 and 547 litres per year. This is enough to fill two standard-sized bathtubs! However, saliva can vary depending on age, diet, hydration levels, and medications.

Fact# 65

The average person takes about 20,000 breaths every day.

Breathing is a necessary life process that involves inhaling oxygen and exhaling carbon dioxide. The average person breathes in and out about 20,000 times a day, which amounts to about 13 pints of air. This number may vary depending on factors such as age, gender, physical activity, and overall health. The human respiratory system is responsible for supplying oxygen to the body's cells and removing carbon dioxide from the body. Without proper breathing, the body cannot function properly, leading to serious health problems. Therefore, paying attention to our breathing and ensuring that we breathe deeply and regularly to maintain good health and well-being is essential.

Fact# 66

Listening to music can synchronize your heart rate and breathing.

Research has shown that the rhythm of music can profoundly affect our bodies, including our heart rate and breathing. As we listen to music, our bodies naturally try to synchronize with the beat, resulting in changes in our physiological responses. This can lead to a decreased heart rate and a deeper, more rhythmic breathing pattern. In fact, some studies have shown that listening to slow, calming music can even help to lower blood pressure and reduce stress levels. So, if you're looking for a way to relax and improve your overall well-being, putting on some soothing tunes might be just the thing for you.

Fact# 67

It is a known fact that during pregnancy, the size of a mother's brain reduces.

During pregnancy, the size of a mother's brain reduces due to a natural process called "synaptic pruning." This process involves eliminating unnecessary or unused neural connections in the brain, allowing for more efficient communication between neurons. It is believed that this process occurs to help prepare the mother for the demands of motherhood, such as being able to detect and respond to her infant's needs. However, it's worth noting that this reduction in brain size is not accompanied by any cognitive decline or adverse effects on the mother's mental abilities. In fact, research has shown that maternal brain changes are associated with increased empathy, improved memory, and enhanced social cognition.

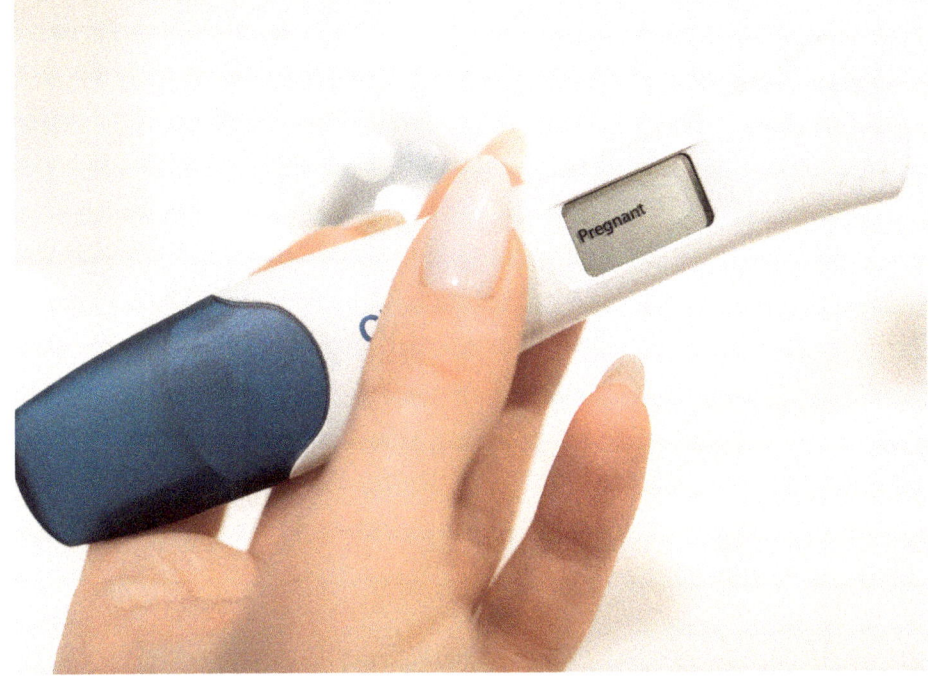

Fact# 68

Did you know sneezing with your eyes open is physically impossible?

When a person sneezes, their body automatically triggers a reflex to close their eyes. This involuntary response occurs due to the stimulation of the trigeminal nerve, which is responsible for controlling the muscles around the eyes and face. The pressure created by a sneeze can cause damage to the eyes or ears if they are not closed, which is why the body has this protective mechanism in place. It is not recommended to forcefully keep your eyes open while sneezing, as it can lead to potential harm.

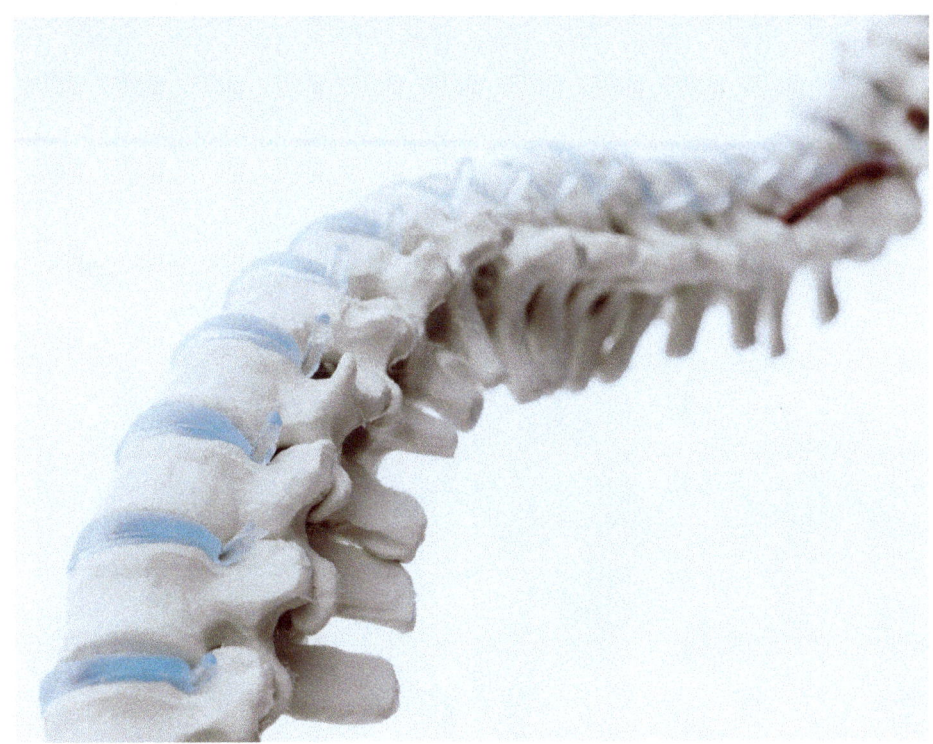

Fact# 69

Do you know dehydration in the body can lead to back pain?

Dehydration can lead to back pain because the spine's intervertebral discs are mostly water. When you become dehydrated, these discs lose their water content and become less flexible and more prone to damage. This can lead to pain and discomfort in the back, especially in the lower back. Also, dehydration can cause muscle cramps and spasms, contributing to back pain. Staying hydrated is vital to keep your back healthy and prevent pain.

Fact# 70

On average, humans have the same number of hairs on their bodies as chimpanzees.

Humans and chimpanzees belong to the same taxonomic family, Hominidae. As a result, they share many similarities in their physical characteristics. One of these similarities is the number of hairs on their bodies. On average, humans have around 5 million hairs on their bodies, which is the same as chimpanzees. However, humans have much less hair on their bodies than other primates like gorillas and orangutans. The reason for this is thought to be related to the evolution of humans as bipedal creatures, which required less hair for protection and warmth. Despite the similarities in the number of hairs, there are differences in hair distribution between humans and chimpanzees. Humans have hair that is more evenly distributed across their bodies, while chimpanzees have thicker hair on their backs and arms and less hair on their chests and stomachs. Overall, the similarity in the number of hairs between humans and chimpanzees is just one of the many interesting biological connections between these two species.

REFERENCES

- http://www.health24.com/lifestyle/woman/your-life/30-weird-medical-facts-20120721

- https://www.verywell.com/disturbing-world-smoking-facts-2825336

- http://oddstuffmagazine.com/50-really-weird-facts-about-your-body.html

- http://www.knowable.com/a/23-fascinating-and-weird-facts-about-the-human-body-wow

- https://www.sleep.org/articles/get-rid-of-sleep-debt/

- https://www.ncoa.org/article/the-truth-about-hydration-7-myths-and-facts

- https://edition.cnn.com/2021/05/05/health/glasses-of-water-per-day-wellness-partner/index.html

- https://www.everydayhealth.com/dehydration/the-truth-about-hydration-myths-and-facts/

- https://athletics.carleton.ca/2015/12-fun-facts-about-exercising/

- https://www.hopkinsmedicine.org/health/wellness-and-prevention/exercising-for-better-sleep

- https://www.healthline.com/nutrition/10-benefits-of-exercise#TOC_TITLE_HDR_7

- https://kidsdiscover.com/quick-reads/human-bodys-smallest-parts/

- https://www.inc.com/john-brandon/25-amazing-facts-about-the-human-brain-you-should-probably-memorize.html

THANK YOU

We extend our heartfelt gratitude for joining us on this captivating journey through the intricacies of the human body. "Human Body Facts for Sharp Minds" was crafted to provide you with an enlightening and visually stimulating exploration of the marvel that is the human body.

We are thankful for the opportunity to share 65 fascinating facts, each accompanied by detailed explanations and vivid illustrations. We aimed to inform and inspire a sense of wonder about the incredible machine that is the human body.

Whether you are a student, a healthcare professional, or someone with a keen interest in the wonders of the human body, we are grateful to have been a part of your intellectual exploration. Your support motivates us to continue creating content that stimulates the mind and encourages a lifelong love for learning.

Thank you for choosing "Human Body Facts for Sharp Minds." We sincerely hope that the knowledge gained from these pages stays with you, sparking conversations, curiosity, and a continual thirst for understanding the world within.

Thank you for choosing and trusting us!

Don't forget to share your experience and give a review.